THE COLLEGE AND UNIVERSITY TRUSTEE

A View from the Board Room

Louis H. Heilbron

THE
COLLEGE
AND
UNIVERSITY
TRUSTEE

Jossey-Bass Publishers
San Francisco • Washington • London • 1973

THE COLLEGE AND UNIVERSITY TRUSTEE
A View from the Board Room
    by Louis H. Heilbron

Copyright © 1973 by: Jossey-Bass, Inc., Publishers
                    615 Montgomery Street
                    San Francisco, California 94111

                    &

                    Jossey-Bass Limited
                    3 Henrietta Street
                    London WC2E 8LU

Library of Congress Catalogue Card Number LC 72-5888

International Standard Book Number ISBN 0-87589-196-9

Manufactured in the United States of America

JACKET DESIGN BY WILLI BAUM

FIRST EDITION

Code 7337

THE
JOSSEY-BASS SERIES
IN HIGHER EDUCATION

Special Advisors

JOSEPH AXELROD
San Francisco State University
University of California, Berkeley

MERVIN B. FREEDMAN
San Francisco State University
and Wright Institute, Berkeley

PREFACE

The College and University Trustee is for trustees, about trustees, by a trustee. It particularly focuses on boards of trustees of public universities and colleges, although trustees of private institutions will find it pertinent and informative, as will also administrators, faculty members, and students, whose activities are affected by the trustee.

Excellent books and commentaries have been written about trusteeship by administrators and a few by trustees whose experience has been principally with private institutions. But the public trustee has been reticent; perhaps because he spends much of his time on view in a glass bowl, he feels that he presents too familiar a picture. Yet he faces unique problems by virtue of his public trust, and it is appropriate that he should express his point of view.

This book seeks to identify and suggest answers to some of these troublesome problems: For whom or for what do the trustees hold the public trust? What is a balanced board and how is it to be achieved? What are the appropriate areas for board policy? How should the board deal with sensitive issues—size of the campus, standards of admission, tenure, discipline, ethnic studies, defense contracts, innovations? What is the academic freedom trustees are called upon to defend? How should the trustees view collective bargaining and what should they do if it comes to their institution?

This book also deals with the basic trustee relationships—with the president, upon whom the board must depend, and with the faculty and students and with their needs and aspirations. Recommendations are made concerning campus speakers and the campus press. The book indicates what trustees should understand and respect in the student culture and what deficiencies they should try to remedy. The external relationships of the trustees are also considered—how they should deal with the budget in relation to the executive and legislative branches, how they should relate to the media and the police, what their attitude should be toward the ever-expanding federal presence and to coordinating boards or super-boards. It considers the core question: How do public college trustees discharge their obligation to the public interest and to the institution itself?

These problems are illustrated by a number of important examples: the Eldridge Cleaver experimental course at the University of California, the *avant-garde* play at Fullerton and exhibit of sculptures at California State College, Long Beach, the Stanford University Bruce Franklin case and its bearing on academic freedom and incitement to violence. My purpose in being specific is to point up the issue. Whether my recommendations concerning these problems are right is not as important as that they stimulate constructive discussion to achieve the appropriate answer for a given institution.

Some matters are made the subject of recommendations, in italic type, at the end of sections. If these recommendations are not always a guide to the perplexed trustee at least they should help him to arrive at his own solution.

A number of incidents referred to occurred in the turbulent Sixties and are not reflected in the quieter waters of the present. But the questions they raised will recur. Student moods and modes change (militancy is out, pragmatism is in); life styles are seldom for life; but the perennial problems of youth's self-realization and adjustment to or revolt against society will always be with us.

My fondest acknowledgements go to my wife, who, though she did not sit like patience on a monument, showed monumental patience while this book was being written. My acknowledgements go also to the many trustees, administrators, faculty members, and students who have educated me in some of the mysterious ways of higher education; to Frank L. Kidner, vice-president, educational relations, University of California, Berkeley, and to William Boyd, president, University of Central Michigan, for their comments on certain parts of the manuscript; to William Langsdorf, academic vice-chancellor, California State University, for making his materials available regarding the case of "The Beard"; and to James G. Paltridge, Center for Research and Development in Higher Education, University of California, Berkeley, for his assistance in providing data.

San Francisco   Louis H. Heilbron
September 1973

CONTENTS

THE COLLEGE
AND
UNIVERSITY TRUSTEE

A View from the Board Room

1

NATURE OF THE TRUST

The college or university trustee is a phenomenon more developed in American higher education than elsewhere. Sometimes called a regent or governor, and sometimes other titles not nearly so complimentary, the trustee is a member of the board legally charged with governing the institution.

His prototype appeared during the Italian Renaissance, when municipalities (city states) took over the management of several universities and elected four or more "good citizens" to oversee the conduct of their institutions and make recommendations to the university rectors. Students had founded these universities, but succeeding generations were not able to guarantee the expenses (principally the salaries of distinguished teachers), and the cities assumed the jurisdiction and the obligation. The existence of the university was a mark of prestige for the city, which often effected rental concessions in order to attract foreign students. Trustees continued in post-Reformation Scottish and Dutch universities as laymen advising or controlling university policy. In the American

1

colonies, because of the importance of religion, it was natural that the administration of church-sponsored institutions (engaged in the training of ministers) should be entrusted to clergymen and lay leaders of the church establishment. Later on, in the nineteenth century, their places were taken by men from the business and professional establishment. Trustees of most of our public institutions, which began to flourish after the Civil War, were also drawn from these groups. Ultimately, almost all American colleges and universities, both private and public, were organized with boards of trustees at the top level, an arrangement probably strengthened by the prevailing form in the burgeoning commerce of the nineteenth century—the corporation controlled by a board of directors.

Now we have thousands of single or multiple institutions—graduate, undergraduate, and community colleges—all with boards of trustees, some with as few as three, others with thirty-five or more. And most of these institutions have adopted *trustee* as the title of the board member.

What has this trustee come to be? What are his functions and powers? Is he a force for good or ill? Is he superfluous? As so often happens, the answer may depend on the bias of the beholder.

From the viewpoint of the administration—the president and deans—he is a personnel problem who requires special handling according to his humor and temperament. But he is also a sounding board, a buffer against pressures from faculty, students, and outside agencies. He is a perpetual student who must be educated by the administration in time to meet a crisis, a fabricator of prefabricated policies.

From the viewpoint of faculty he is a meddler in educational affairs, a possible vehicle for overturning the administration and transferring its authority to the faculty; a dubious court of last resort in disciplinary cases; an agent to procure the appropriations the faculty wants; a man with a corporate bias who seeks to run the college like a business; sometimes a kind and friendly soul who might be brought to the door of the temple but who should never be allowed to enter or to share the secrets of the brotherhood.

From the viewpoint of students, he is a member of the older generation who usually cannot understand, often immobilized by tradition, ocassionally preoccupied with hair and hang-ups, a symbol of the establishment; actually, no more harmful than Dad, and surprisingly one who can be talked to when protesting requirements and asking for change.

From the viewpoint of other trustees, he is a pretty good fellow (though he may be a little too talkative or too taciturn or too liberal or too conservative); interested only in a better educational program; wanting to do a fair, honest, constructive job; unhappy when there is friction in the college community; willing to cooperate with all parties; expecting no public thanks and, in this respect, not being disappointed.

The key part of the trustee's title is (or should be) the word *trust*. He holds something valuable in trust—the classrooms, the libraries, the laboratories, the dormitories, the complex interrelationship of students and faculty, the institution itself—for high purposes and benefits, not for himself, but for others.

But for whom? Students, radical and moderate, contend that the trust exists for students—that they are the sole intended beneficiaries during their college life and that the next appropriate beneficiaries are the next college generation. They believe their desires and directions for a "relevant" academic course must control. The career-oriented must be accorded their choice of training. The ethnic students must define their study content and objectives. The mystic and escapist students must have the opportunity to do their thing. The beneficiaries want to define the trust.

Faculty support the idea that the institution exists for its students, but many faculty, particularly in the research-oriented institutions, believe that, to a substantial extent, they should be the beneficiaries of the trust. The principal function of the university is to explore the frontiers of knowledge and produce new knowledge; the faculty are the pioneers on this frontier, and the institution should support their ventures and explorations. While it is true that knowledge is discovered for the ultimate benefit of society or mankind, it is nevertheless implied that many immediate and practical benefits redound to the researcher when his work is financially supported—therefore, the claim that the trust is partly for the benefit of the faculty.

Frequently the trust is declared to be for the benefit of society, state, and nation. The more the state has supported higher education, the argument goes, the more productive and affluent its society has become. The development of California agriculture is largely the result of University of California research and dissemination of the results to the farmers and farming interests of California. The location of the new industries of electronics and technology has been determined largely by the location of existing facilities of higher learning that produce many engineers and scientifically trained personnel. Most top and middle management of industry have come from higher education institutions. And, increasingly in the last forty years, the top echelons of government have always included advisors and administrators taken or borrowed from our leading universities.

If the best citizen is the informed citizen and if knowledge is power, then today's higher education, with its higher enrollments, should contribute much to the American body politic. Certainly the stake of society in higher education has become increasingly clear. Yet recent years of campus unrest have produced disillusionment that has caused some political and social leaders to question whether higher education is fulfilling its trust for society and the state.

In private institutions the charter or trust declared by the original donor of the institution theoretically governs its trustees. However, many of these institutions were created in prior centuries, and their original purposes have been either liberally construed or quietly forgotten in order to meet the needs of the times, indeed, in order to survive.

In the broader sense the trustee's trust is to perpetuate our heritage for present and future generations. But we must be careful not to limit the scope of trust purposes. While unquestionably the university exists to preserve the best of Western civilization, it is concerned with all civilization and with changing civilizations. Higher education deals with all ideas and all stages of being, past, present, and future. It studies and theorizes and forewarns regarding the future. It can help us prepare for the future.

Indeed, the purposes of the universities and colleges are too broad to be limited to any particular group or concept—students, faculty, the existing state, or the present civilization. There are permanent and passing elements in the purposes of higher education. As we shall see in Chapter Four, the trust of the trustee is to implement long- and short-term educational goals to the full extent that his particular institution or system of institutions is in a position to do so. In a word, the trust is to provide that governance that will best carry out the purposes of higher education as applied to a particular institution or group of institutions.

It should be noted that the public trust has a special character. The citizen taxpayers believe they are entitled, as trustors supporting the institution, to voice their views to the trustees on the conduct of the institution and to expect that proper attention will be paid to them. Faculty and students may demand that the trustees protect the "independence" of the institution against the pressures of the public. Are public trustees committed to the town or to the gown? The answer is that they have obligations to both. They must be concerned with their respective protests. If the trustees can persuade the institution to be true to its purposes and the town to honor these purposes, they will be acting in the interests of both parties. In a tense situation this is more easily said than done.

2

BALANCED
BOARD

In most private institutions, boards are self-perpetuating; they fill
their own vacancies. Few board members resign, so a trustee has a
life career. The deficiency in this procedure is that it promotes
inertia, too much single-minded experience, too many old members,
and too few new ideas. The board of trustees of Columbia University discovered this fact too late in their encounter with students to
save the university from the bitter strife of the spring of 1968.

In other ways, public institutions have not fared much better.
Usually the governor has the determining voice in selecting trustees
for the state universities and colleges. Sometimes the consent of the
upper house of the state legislature is required, but it is usually
given as a matter of courtesy. (However, in 1972 the California
Senate withheld its consent for several months in two instances,
reportedly because it felt new State University trustees mirrored too
much the economic and social backgrounds of the existing trustees.)
Terms vary greatly; the average is about six years in senior institutions, although they may run as much as sixteen years. The choices

for board membership are likely to reflect the governor's political philosophy. Where board terms run up to eight years, a twice-elected governor can appoint all the members of the board. It also can happen that successive governors with opposing educational philosophies can, through their appointees, provide polarized and somewhat frustrated boards for a substantial period of time.

Both the private and public boards call for reform in the method and conditions of appointment. Here are some of the more important considerations for public boards.

Selection and Terms

For balance and continuity, trustee terms should be staggered. But how long should these terms be? Not so long that a trustee becomes stale on the job or loses his enthusiasm for the challenge. Not so short that he cannot use his growth in the job to the advantage of the institution. Certainly his term should be long enough so that he can act free from political influence.

No fool-proof mathematical formula is available for determining the proper term. In California, a citizens' select committee reviewing the state's master plan for higher education recommended a single term of twelve years, with room for a prior appointment for a portion of an expired term. Such a period, it was believed, would afford optimum opportunities for experience, independence from political pressures, and—in a board of twelve or more—annual turnover to admit new blood. A special California legislative committee, engaged in a similar study, proposed eight years (renewable) as the proper term.

Perhaps a completely different approach should be taken in determining length of terms. If the purpose is to remove the trustee from the danger of political influence, then it may be preferable to provide for shorter, medium-length terms (six to eight years), but there should be a procedure of selection that would ensure more consistency in the quality of appointments. This result can be achieved by the creation of a special advisory commission on appointments.

This commission may be constituted in several ways. One possibility is a commission of fourteen members, with six official and eight citizen members.[1] The legislative voice would be represented by the president of the state senate and speaker of the state assembly or, alternatively, by the chairman of the education committee of each legislative house. The chairman of the entire commission would be the chief justice of the state supreme court or his designee. Other ex-officio members would include the chairman of the statewide agency whose board was involved in the appointment, the chairman of that institution's statewide academic senate, and a student representative chosen by a council of student body presidents of the campuses represented in that agency.

The majority of the commission would be citizen members (including alumni), four to be appointed by the legislature and four by the governor. These citizen members would be appointed for four-year terms. (For the initial term, half of those selected as decided by lot would serve for only two years, thereby providing for staggered terms.) The members would be drawn from both major political parties; not less than one-third would be from one of these parties.

This commission would present three to five nominations for each appointment, from which the governor would choose one; there would be no senate confirmation. (A joint legislative committee in California has proposed that a nominating committee representative of the legislature, governing boards, faculty, alumni, and students propose five to ten persons for each vacancy, but this number seems excessive.) The term of the trustee would be from six to eight years, with the possibility of one renewal; however, the filling out of any unexpired term for more than two years should count as a single term.

This proposal is an adaption of the 1972 recommendation to the California legislature by President Charles J. Hitch of the University of California. He urged the continuance of a sixteen-year term for University of California regents or, as the alternative, an advisory procedure for appointment of regents much as outlined above.

If it is a state tradition that the governor consults educa-

---

[1] The control by the appointed citizen members is the important factor. A commission consisting mostly of legislative and executive officials would defeat the purpose of such a body as nonpartisan and nonpolitical.

tional leadership and chooses mostly from their nominations, then an elaborate, formal nominating procedure may not be necessary. Moreover, if a board consists equally of members representing the two major political parties, as is required for the University of Kentucky, this may accomplish the purposes of nonpartisanship.

Actually, if the term is sufficiently long, experience indicates that political influence is not such an important factor even though a single governor may have appointed all or a majority of the trustees. After a few years, the trustee becomes immersed in the problems of the institution which it is his duty to govern. If he does not have to be concerned about being reappointed, he tends to take an independent position even against the governor who may have appointed him. This parallels the experience of judges. More than one President or governor has been surprised by the decisions of the justice whom he appointed to a life term. However, if the shorter term is preferred for historic reasons or because it seems to provide more responsiveness to the needs for change, then some kind of procedure for screened nominations appears advisable.

Terms of appointive trustee boards should be staggered and should be sufficiently long to encourage independent action. A single term of twelve years seems optimum for appointments by a governor (with confirmation by the state senate). Adoption of this principle would require substantial changes in most boards since the average term now is about six years.

Another approach is to have a blue-ribbon panel, chaired by the chief justice of the state supreme court, nominate three or more candidates for each vacancy, with trustees appointed by the governor to six- to eight-year terms.

Election

Elected board members are another alternative. Trustees of a junior college district governing board are usually elected by the voters of that district, who have some opportunity to meet and know the candidates. It is less usual to elect trustees of statewide institutions. There are, however, some exceptions—for instance, the University of Michigan, Michigan State University, Wayne State University, and the University of Colorado. In the Michigan institutions mentioned, the elected boards are chosen for eight-year terms, and two members are subject to election every two years. Trustees are nominated by political party caucuses. Traditionally both parties have nominated able and distinguished men for regents of the University of Michigan, but apparently the other two universities have not fared so well. Michigan State trustees are reported to be in a constant state of partisan and ideological debate, and the Wayne State board is emerging from a period of similar strife. Obviously, unless the political parties act as conscientious screening agencies, the representation on a statewide elective board will be uneven and unsatisfactory.

One difficulty with party selection not shaped by a controlling tradition is that disappointed candidates for other offices may be thrown a trusteeship as a consolation prize. Another problem is that the principle of balanced representation is not given much effect in the process. The overriding consideration is that it is often difficult to obtain trustees free of partisan political influences through selection by the party structures.

The University of Nebraska, University of Colorado, and several southern universities elect on a congressional, regental, or other district basis; the boards are usually small, with six to nine trustees, and probably are no more or less distinguished than the general run of boards elected on a statewide basis. Party nominees run on "platforms" of "reform" or otherwise and commit themselves to programs before they know what the job is about.

Election of trustees on a nonpartisan statewide basis would produce other complications. Leading representatives of the type desired would not be interested in becoming candidates. Those who would run for office would be likely to reflect the positions of whatever organizations provided the funds for their candidacies. Furthermore, it would be almost impossible to expect that such trustees would achieve the desired balance of commitment and representation.

As far as obtaining trustees responsive to the public interest, election is certainly the most democratic procedure, but democratic controls can also be sufficiently safeguarded through the appointment process and the powers over finance and appropriation reserved to the governor and legislature.

If the electoral process is used to select board members, then there must be machinery for nominations through strong alumni associations and other organizations such as party caucuses under responsible leaders committed to education.

Age and Number

Seventy seems a reasonable age limitation for trustees. Because most administrators and faculty must retire by that time, there is no reason to except trustees. Some wisdom will be sacrificed by applying such a policy, but some senility and a great deal of embarrassment will be avoided. Enthusiasm and fresh attitudes should result from appointing more than a token number of members under the age of forty (including any students), and a national movement in this direction is now under way.

The number of board members varies with the institution. To be representative, there should be no less than eleven for smaller institutions and no more than twenty-four, even for larger institutions. These figures are not magic numbers; less than eleven, with faithful attendance, may function successfully, and more than twenty-four may still operate without being too cumbersome: I have seen a board of thirty-five do well, but only because the procedure was highly formalized and structured.

The board of any institution should be of such size that it can gather at one table (circular, square, rectangular, or horseshoe), to allow for the representation of necessary constituencies and to permit free-flowing discussion. The desideratum must be determined in the light of probable attendance. Thus, a board of twenty-one, with a usual attendance of eleven, may prove marginal in size related to responsibility.

Chronic absenteeism (unless for some specially excusable circumstance which looks toward a full resumption of duties) should be strictly dealt with under rule or policy. A nonattendant trustee is not fulfilling his trust and should be removed or requested to resign under conditions that would make it embarrassing for him to refuse.

Seventy is a reasonable retirement age for trustees. The board should consist of enough members so that representative points of view may be considered and expressed and so that a quorum (majority of members) will not be too small. I have sug-gested that there be not less than eleven (though many boards have less) or more than twenty-four members.

"Establishment" Trustees

As indicated, the nature of board representation may affect size. What kind of people should make up a board? Until recently, this was not a plausible question. It was accepted that successful businessmen and professional men—prepared to offer their expertise, knowledgeable in the way things get done in the marketplace, and motivated to contribute financially to the cause of education—were the only appropriate candidates for trusteeship. But faculty members, students, alumni, ethnic groups, and women's liberationists have called attention to themselves as other areas from which necessary and valuable representation can be drawn.

Consider the establishment representatives. They should not be selected merely because they may occupy strategic executive positions in the community. They should have demonstrated an understanding of and interest in higher education. For the most part they should be the products of higher education, but it would be a mistake to exclude a self-educated man whose understanding of the educational purpose may be greater than that of a graduate with a degree.

Some faculty and students oppose the idea of substantial establishment representation, believing that the institution cannot then respond to student needs and new life styles and that such representation merely widens the generation gap. My experience indicates that sometimes these trustees are more willing than faculty to listen to students. And it must be remembered that establishment trustees are leaders of the society that supports the institution, and that successful performance and recognition in society may well indicate an ability to contribute to the most crucial institution serving it.

Moreover, valuable expertise becomes available to the institution at little or no cost. The financial expert can be most helpful in recommending policies that will redound to the benefit of the university's investment portfolio; the architect can help develop policies that will protect the institution in making the best and most esthetic use of the investment dollar; the lawyer can keep discussions to the issue and try to ensure clear and consistent drafts of policy resolutions and statements; and the publisher can be helpful by being sensitive to the manner in which policies are stated or announced. Yet, there are dangers too in the exercise of expertise: the physician may want to dictate health decisions, the lawyer may cause undue qualification and technical debate, and the architect may insist on scrapping all plans and starting anew. The rest of the board must beware of an expert member who is too aggressive and opinionated in a matter affecting his specialty.

Labor is a part of the establishment these days, and the representative from labor can contribute considerably to the development of sound personnel policies and relationships. However, one problem does arise in the event of collective bargaining, particularly if some form of it is adopted for academic employees. There may be times when the labor representative finds himself in a conflicting situation between management (as a governing board member) and labor. But his interest and sympathy for labor should be understood and expected by his colleagues. He can help them evaluate a difficult situation by assuming the adversary point of view. He may also be able to have an impact on union demands and techniques because he will understand the financial and other pertinent problems of the institution. If the conflict places him in an untenable position, he will normally excuse himself or abstain. I have seen this occur on several occasions.

If it is possible to generalize with respect to qualifications for a board member, I would suggest a person of intelligence, decency, and compassion; a person with some important previous experience in education; an achiever in his field not limited to earnings or wealth but including community service; usually a college graduate, so that he or she has a frame of reference; a person of moral standards but not a zealous moralist; a person who respects the teaching profession; one who is genuinely concerned about youth and youth's future; a person who need not be of all seasons but certainly living in the present, not the past, and one willing to listen and to decide.

All board members should possess high personal qualifica-

tions. Trustees should always include substantial membership from the establishment with experience in education and community service. As leaders of the society supporting the institution, they can gain support for it and can make available their expertise for little or no cost.

Alumni, Women, Minorities

Alumni have a tie to their institution which is unique. They are frequently its major financial supporters or lobbyists for funds. They are familiar with the university or college scene; they have been "through it"; they have a framework of reference when campus problems arise. If they are organized and constitute a vigorous and effective group, it is natural that they should be represented on the board, even apart from the selection of other board members who also may be alumni of the institution. The president of the alumni association should hold a trusteeship during the period of his office as alumni president.

Most boards of trustees are exclusively male. Yet the student bodies in most colleges and universities are coeducational, and in many of them the number of women students exceeds the number of men students. In the few institutions that have remained women's colleges, the board of trustees nevertheless has a substantial male representation.

It makes no sense to exclude women from boards of trustees. There should be substantial women's representation on almost every board. The record of women on boards is interesting. In matters affecting issues of morals and mores, they tend to be ahead of the men and on the liberal side. For instance, men are much more likely to resist the establishment of coeducational dormitories than women, who, when they see the inevitable, tend to accept it.

Almost all institutions now have affirmative admissions policies for minority students. Eligibility rules are relaxed in order to extend opportunities to the educationally disadvantaged, although minorities in urban centers often contend that these rules have not been sufficiently modified—that they are still grounded in racial bias and must be changed in order materially to increase the percentage of minority enrollments and opportunity. Moreover, minority students, after admission, have demonstrated their own particular concerns and problems.

In the light of these considerations it is clear that persons from minority groups should be on boards of trustees in order to assist in the deliberations concerning minority problems. Of course, such representatives should be selected on the basis of their also being able to share an overall view of the institution's affairs and purposes. Persons from service fields such as social welfare and from community organizations may also make effective trustees.

Alumni, women, and minorities should be represented on the board as a matter of fairness and right and also because of the special contributions they can make to the welfare of the institution: alumni for general and financial support; women to balance the male outlook; and minority members to give informed views on admission and education problems.

Faculty

Since a university consists essentially of students and faculty, their demands that they participate in policy determination are understandable. But the way these aspirations are recognized is also important, for a trustee (whoever he may be) must accept his trust for the entire institution.

A board of trustees needs to hear the viewpoint of faculty, requires the input and participation of faculty, in connection with most of its policy decisions. But this participation may be better achieved through a formalized procedure whereby the official faculty body presents its position at a board meeting rather than through board representation. That is, members of the official board of the faculty's academic senate should be present at every meeting of the trustees and be expected to participate in the discussion of any policy affecting faculty interests, educational policy, or the welfare of the institution. The official faculty group can then assume a position of advocacy more easily than can a faculty representative on the board.

The determining factor may be status, not effectiveness. If

the faculty knows that certain of its members are actually part of the final decision-making authority, it may be more supportive of and cooperative with the board's decisions. From the standpoint of trustees, the problem of faculty representation is whether the faculty-member trustee represents a constituency or the entire institution. Normally, trustees do not consider themselves obligated to any particular group or sector of the university or of the community; they may be constrained by their own background or biases, but not by an organized segment inside or outside the institution. (I except those few trustees of a public institution who will blindly follow any directions given by the governor who appointed them.) Will the faculty trustee take a narrow, faculty "minority" point of view on university issues? Will he be compelled to do so by the pressure of his organized colleagues? Finally, does the appointment of a faculty member to the board place the president or chancellor in an embarrassing position because one of his "employees" is also his boss?

There are practical answers to all of these questions. A recently retired professor or a professor from another institution would be relatively immune to local academic pressure, yet he would bring the academic experience and viewpoint to the board. If the appointing power—board or governor—were to select the faculty representatives, the probabilities are that a militant leader for "faculty power" would not be appointed. But an appointee of a nonfaculty authority might not be accepted by the faculty as being truly representative; he would always be suspect as a "company man." If board membership is to be extended to campus faculty, it is better that the representatives come directly from faculty choice, either by special election or by ex officio membership (with voting power) resulting from their election to positions of leadership in the official faculty body (senate or assembly) and perhaps in a professional school. It seems advisable that at least two faculty members be chosen, otherwise the system will be accused of tokenism. (It may be anyway.)

The experience of administrators who have dealt with combined faculty-administrative councils, or combined faculty-student-administrative councils, is that they adopt an overall institutional view after the first meeting, if not immediately. In other words, the fear that a "constituency" attitude toward problems of the institution would prevail, by reason of the faculty representation, does not appear to be the likely or necessary result. On a campus dominated by a cadre of academic politicians or by a militantly activist faculty, the contrary may be true; that is, faculty representatives may be expected to follow a constituency line. In this situation, it would be understandable if the board were reluctant to accept faculty participation.

Of course, even under normal circumstances, there are times when the broadest-gauged faculty representative would be expected to act with particular faculty interests in mind. For example, if the subject is a faculty pay increase, it is difficult to imagine circumstances when the faculty representative would not support it or contend for it, and close to the maximum amount feasible. Certainly, such a position would be understood by his board colleagues. But his knowledge of the fiscal condition of the institution and its other obligations and commitments derived through participation in the board discussions may well cause him to adjust his viewpoint with respect to what amount is realistic and appropriate. Moreover, with his disciplined mind, a faculty member should be able to recommend reasonable solutions to such questions, even though they are close to the interests of himself and his faculty colleagues. Finally, it should be remembered that faculty representatives would be only a fraction of the board and could not prevail against a substantial majority vote.

One qualification is in order. If the salary and other conditions of faculty work are determined through collective bargaining or similar process, then faculty representation on a board seems to present very difficult problems. Faculty, to a substantial extent, then become employees of the institution in a more conventional sense denoting an employer-employee relationship. Under such circumstances the faculty member on the board would be both employer and employee, negotiating on behalf of administration and management in an adversary relationship to his own constituency. When collective bargaining applies, it is doubtful whether faculty representation on the board is even feasible because the needs and aspirations of the constituency would penetrate many substantive matters, and the faculty member would find himself in a series of conflicting-interest situations. A noncampus faculty member might remain, although it could prove awkward if he has any organizational affiliation.

Faculty may have a greater effect on policy by having their representatives attend board meetings as advocates of faculty positions rather than through board membership. If faculty member trustees are preferred, they may be selected from recently retired professors or professors from other institutions. If they are campus faculty, they should be determined by faculty choice. Unionization would change the picture.

Students

Student membership on a board presents some of the same problems as faculty membership. There may be bias toward or control by a constituency, this time the student constituency. Can the student take the larger view? The same question is raised regarding the procedure of selection—by the governor, by the board, by special election, or by ex officio right of student office. And the same answers seem applicable: on an institutional level, students usually take an all-campus view; but to be acceptable as representatives of other students, they should be selected by the students, not the board. Furthermore, on certain student issues, such as student rights in disciplinary cases, they can be counted on to take a "constituency" position. None of these considerations need prevent student representation; the input of the student point of view at the decision-making level may be most valuable in enabling the board to establish policies that will deal constructively with student problems and avoid confrontations and violence.

On the other side, there is the same argument that instead of board membership the students may prefer the right to be present and to comment upon or propose policies at board meetings. In this way, student input can be ensured yet independence is protected—students would not be "compromised" by board membership.

But there are special considerations relating to possible student membership. While faculty have long-term interests in the institution, students are relative transients, and their interests may change materially in a single student generation: compare students of 1960–64 with those of 1964–68 and with those of the present. Sometimes their leadership is impulsive and immature. They can be subject to great influence and pressure from their peers; on occasion they may find it nearly impossible to exercise independent judgment. And if in addition the student elected is a hard-core militant, bent on the destruction of the institution he is supposed to help govern, student representation could approach the impossible. The board would be compelled to share its counsels for the protection of the institution with those who seek to tear it down.

There is also the question of the nature of the student relationship to the institution. Is he an inmate? ("You don't turn over the government of the asylum to the inmates, nor of the hospitals to the patients.") Is he a consumer? ("You don't turn over the government of Macy's to the customers.") Is he a beneficiary? ("He should be grateful for all the things we give him.") Take any of these positions (as boards do) and the conclusion may be that the student has no place on a governing board. It is of interest here that the attorney general in Michigan has advised that a student may not serve on a public college board because of an inherent conflict in interest: he cannot be a governor of an institution that sets the standards for and awards his degree. Such a rule, be it noted, could also exclude the university president because the board sets his salary and conditions of office.

But is the student in fact an inmate, consumer, or beneficiary? He may live in a college dormitory, but he is more than a resident and in no sense is he a ward or an inmate of an institution. He may consume courses by the dozen, but it is a different intake than the material necessities of life; he does benefit from the institution, but subsequently society benefits from him. He is in a kind of joint venture with the institution and society; the knowledge he obtains and the attitudes he develops in the institution may have a profound effect on society later on.

The student can properly point to the early beginnings of universities in Italy, France, and England to prove that he has a historic right to participate in the governance of his institution, though he may wish to omit a reference to South America, where student control of universities has been an educational disaster be-

cause student political and personal interests have dominated both educational content and procedure. Participation on some reasonable basis offers educational advantages to a student; when he must vote on an all-university issue he discovers the meaning of responsibility. Giving students a voice is not transferring control. Student participation on the board may lead to improved communication between generations and more realistic policies concerning students. The number and eligibility should be limited in order to obtain responsible student membership. There are at least three ways of doing this: limit board membership to one or two ex officio student officers with one-year terms, select leadership from responsible student agencies such as honor and service societies, or use a system of nominations from various student groups with final selection by a combined student-faculty-administrative committee (the last the least promising alternative if student representation is to be credible to the student body.)[2]

Like faculty, students may have a greater effect on policy by having their official representatives (not as board members) present student positions at board meetings. If student board members are preferred, they should be students selected from student government or other responsible student organizations.

Public Officials

In many state-supported systems of higher education, public officials by law are often made ex officio trustees—usually the state's governor, lieutenant-governor, possibly a superintendent of public instruction, and the speaker of the assembly or the state controller. The theory of this representation is that it should help the educational institutions, for the public officials represented would then recognize the contributions, problems, and needs of the state's universities and colleges. Moreover, the entire activity of the university or college board is supposed to be nonpartisan and nonpolitical.

[2] Boards of trustees are still resistant both to faculty and to student membership. In 1973 a nationwide poll by the Association of Governing Boards of Universities and Colleges showed that 69 percent of eight hundred board chairmen who responded to the poll were opposed to faculty membership, 68 percent to student representation. The association consists of trustees of public and private institutions.

But since higher education has become a mass program, involving a large share of the state budget, since campus unrest has become front-page news, since Kent State became the symbol of a national calamity, the presence of public officials as trustees has acquired political overtones not present earlier. Elected officials are in a position to exercise an undue amount of control over a board. Under prevaling conditions a governor may appoint a number of trustees whose loyalty he may command when he seeks to adopt a given policy. All these public officials have legitimate political concerns and ambitions, and in the case of a large issue involving public education they usually can be expected to take the popular side, although the unpopular side may be more in line with educational values. Public officials are also more experienced in the use of news media and have easy access to it, while other trustees who may have disagreed with them at the board table have no such expertise or access. Many of the very same officials who will take a firm line against politicizing the campus will not hesitate to politicize the board.[3]

These comments are not made in a spirit of criticizing any particular individual actions. They are made because the public official is often placed in an almost impossible position as far as the welfare of the institution is concerned, when he expresses himself as part of the board on a controversial issue involving higher education. Public officials do have interests and important functions with respect to higher education. The budgets of public institutions are subject to the support and review of the governor; it is usually his authority that must be exercised if, for example, the National Guard is to be called to a campus in order to deal with campus violence. But the actions of the governor and other officials with respect to higher education should be in their capacity as constitutional officers or elected public officials; they should not take the lead in influencing decisions on educational problems at the board level. A lay-appointed board, the Carnegie Commission agrees, should be free from the sometimes overpowering influence of elected public officials.

[3] Perhaps an exception should be made in the case of a nonpartisan official like the State Superintendent of Public Schools. But nonpartisan offices are not always filled by nonpartisan officials.

On balance it seems preferable to exclude ex officio public officials from board membership.

Liberal or Conservative?

Statistical analyses are incomplete in showing what boards do. For example, an unpublished survey by the Center for Research and Development in Higher Education at the University of California, Berkeley, found in a representative sample of twenty-three institutions that 50 percent of trustee decisions are in finance and management, 15 percent in educational policy, and 3 percent in student affairs. But in my personal experience a single decision in the academic area or in student affairs may take a morning or the greater part of a day. To measure the *number* of decisions may not significantly reflect the time devoted to each of them. Moreover, the same survey found that the average number of decisions per meeting for 1971–72 was thirty-plus, but this fact does not reveal anything about substance or quality.

Also Hartnett[4] in 1969 supplied considerable data to prove that most trustees, on both private and public boards, were white, Protestant, affluent, and between fifty and sixty years of age. However, it appears to me that the attitudes expressed by a majority of them on a number of substantive issues reported by him lean toward the liberal side. They believed, for example, that faculty members have the right to free expression of opinions, that students should control the contents of student newspapers, that the institution should help solve social problems, that opportunities should be available for anyone wanting higher education, that the curriculum should be designed to serve a diverse student body. The older and younger members separately made up these majorities. On procedural questions (such as of sharing authority with faculty and students) boards of nonselective institutions, particularly open-enrollment institutions such as junior colleges, tended to be con-

[4] Rodney T. Hartnett, *College and University Trustees: Their Backgrounds Roles, and Educational Attitudes* (Princeton, N.J.: Educational Texting Service, 1969). See also Rodney T. Hartnett, "Trustee Power in America," in Harold L. Hodgkinson and L. Richard Meeth, eds., *Power and Authority,* (San Francisco: Jossey-Bass, 1971).

servative and to cling to authority. Thus, the establishment makeup of a board does not necessarily indicate liberal or conservative action, though in either case it is no argument against broadening representation. What it does suggest is that establishment trustees are not conservative stereotypes.

As of 1973, studies were being conducted at the University of California to determine whether boards of diversified representation act differently from establishment boards. Assuming responsible membership in each case, the records may not prove to be as different as might be anticipated. The case for the diversified board is not that its decisions will be greatly changed but that it will symbolize greater equality of opportunity and that its decisions will be more credible to various segments of the academic community and the public.

3

BOARD
ADMINISTRATION

Not many years ago, if you received a letter asking you to become a college trustee, you would probably have accepted without much concern. You might have asked if the duties were onerous and would have been assured the contrary. Meetings, held every six or eight weeks, would be congenial and would give you a chance to renew old and pleasant associations, visit Ivy Hall, and hear the president report on the state of the college. And, of course, you would have preferential seats at football games and occasionally perhaps be able to exchange greetings with a Nobel Laureate. Being a trustee was primarily an honor—and neither hazardous nor burdensome, for it was the president who ran the institution.

If you receive the same invitation today, you would do well to consider before replying. First of all, you had better be prepared to work. Monthly or periodic meetings are only the beginning—there will be committees and luncheon conferences and telephone calls. Second, you may have to decide on some sticky issues on student protest and faculty discipline and to respond to the pressures of concerned alumni, public officials, and citizen groups. Third, the

24

honor of your position will be recognized only in serving it to the best of your conscience and ability and not in any public acclaim or approval.

Meetings and Committees

There will be monthly, possibly bimonthly, regular meetings, occasional special meetings, and committee meetings. Where will they take place? Usually, if it is the board of a single institution, you will meet on campus (although if the campus is in the heat of controversy, the board may determine that it is in the best interests of all concerned to meet in the nearest city or town).

A board cannot operate successfully as a committee of the whole; it is more effective when it creates committees to perform special chores. One committee often formed is an executive committee to act for the board between meetings. This arrangement works better in private than public institutions, because usually for important actions public institutions require a quorum of the board to determine official action. Beyond this there is also the danger that the executive committee may become a tight, small in-group that will allocate to itself the determination of most board policies, so that the activities of the board generally become nominal. This is not good for board morale or effectiveness, and it can frustrate the objective of a representative board. Occasionally an executive committee is useful, but the concept should be approached with considerable caution. A board will gain in cohesiveness and in its sense of responsibility if it deals as a whole with the major policy questions.

As for other committees, the functions of the board should determine their scope. Certainly educational policy is an overriding concern and should be the subject of one of the committees, however specifically designated. Faculty and staff affairs are a natural committee grouping for dealing with personnel questions and relationships with faculty bodies. Other logical committees are budget or finance; external affairs, including fund procurement; plant and equipment, involving capital expenditures and expansion. Standing committees may or may not be required for student affairs, minority admissions, and employment, although ad hoc committees may be used to deal with special issues as they arise. Sometimes the most effective method of handling a general new issue is to appoint an ad hoc committee consisting of the chairmen of the standing committees. Such a committee is particularly useful in dealing with a complex issue which touches upon most of the operations of the institution.

Boards of single institutions should usually meet on campus. Boards generally should organize their investigative work through committees but avoid creating an executive committee that would make major policy decisions.

Chairman

The chairman is the board officer with whom the college president will have most of his relationships. The chairman should be an experienced trustee with deep commitments to the institution and should understand that the president and not the lay chairman is the educator and the principal source of policy. He can give valuable guidance to the president in many areas: in dealing with public and community personalities, in giving the background history of the institution, and in indicating the chief concerns of the board. In addition, the chairman can make his own contributions to the institution, especially in bringing to the attention of the administration and the board the interests of the community and in focusing the board's attention on matters of policy as distinguished from administrative detail.

The chairman must not be a competitor of the president, and in the interest of the institution he should not attempt to dominate it. Indeed, if a college presidential candidate discovers that the chairman insists upon exercising the powers of the president, that he is in fact a frustrated president, the candidate should not accept the job, for it would be an unhappy struggle. A president should be flexible, however, for he will probably serve under several chairmen.

It is better that this should occur. A strong board will always have a number of personalities who can lead it, and the chairmanship should rotate every two or three years. One year is too short; the chairman barely ascertains the needs of the post. In the second year he functions much more effectively. Sometimes the requirements of the institution or his capable and enthusiastic leadership may carry him through a third year, but this should be all. The chairman should serve, not remain; other members of the board with fresh viewpoints and enthusiasm should carry on. But one qualification of a chairman should be his ability to relate to the president, unless he is elected for the very purpose of severing that relationship.

The president should inform the chairman of all important developments in the institution. If a serious problem arises, the chairman should be told first; he should not be surprised with it at the board meeting. The president will, in fact, wish to know the possible board reactions to a new policy problem, and it can be to his advantage to use the chairman as a sounding of the board.

The chairman is the presiding officer of the board, but he should not be the principal voice at the board meeting. He should encourage his colleagues to participate to the fullest extent, and he should guide the discussion in the sense of keeping it relevant to the issues. In a matter of great importance to the institution he should not hesitate to express his viewpoint, but he should restrict the use of the prestige of his office to the times when such use is necessary.

After action is taken, however, the chairman must be the spokesman for the board. He should represent it to the press and other media if board expression, in addition to the president's, is requested or is advisable. Trustees should not speak individually on behalf of the board; this is the chairman's function. Sometimes a trustee is asked to comment to the press with respect to his view as contrasted with that of the board majority; of course, the trustee should respond, giving his own view as distinguished from the board's.

There are occasions when one of the committee chairmen may be authorized to speak on behalf of his committee or of the board when it has adopted his committee's recommendations. Whenever possible, this should be done with the consent of the board chairman in order to keep the lines of communication clear.

The chairman is the leader and spokesman of the trustees, but he should not be a competitor of the president.

Agenda

The most important single document before the trustees is the agenda. This innocent-appearing outline of topics may tell the whole story of the effectiveness of the administration and of the board. If the agenda consists of tepid subjects at a time when the institution is seething with difficulties, something is wrong. The board is being ignored or circumvented, and it is the president who is responsible because he produces the agenda.

Some presidents do not wish to burden the trustees with controversial questions or policies, particularly if they must be discussed in a public meeting. The chief executive may want to spare the board or the institution the embarrassment of revealing that not all is going well. This is a grievous error. A board, if it is to perform constructively for the institution, must know the problems that beset it. Also, the board should know that when it receives the policy problem, along with the president's recommendation, the matter has been considered by the interested official segments of the college and that their input is reflected in the recommendation or is adequately represented in the comments of the president. If there is a question of primary interest to faculty, such as the adoption of a new calendar or a statement of due process for faculty discipline, then the official faculty position with respect to these matters must be known along with the president's recommendation. The board has the right to know that the lines of communication within the institution have been used in order to develop sound policy. This does not mean that the president should recommend policies affecting a group in the college with only its consent and approval, but it does mean he should consult with that group before the recommendation is made.

Sometimes the president (or his protective assistant) will place the most controversial issues toward the end of the agenda on the assumption that after one or two days of meeting the board will be tired and will approve the recommendation, even if it is controversial, with a minimum of discussion. Meanwhile, the board has been enmeshed in the detail of routine matters.

On the face of it, this is not a good idea. Important issues, especially those likely to cause debate, should be placed near the beginning of the agenda, when the board is fresh and when the best consideration can be given. An intelligent chairman will have no difficulty dealing with a reversed-priorities agenda. He will simply call for the agenda items out of order, taking the important and controversial questions first. The president will catch on; future agendas will reflect the proper priorities. (The president may not have been directly involved in the preparation of the original agenda.)

Indeed, the chairman would do well to inquire with respect to the agenda items prior to the circulation of the agenda. In his review he can provide valuable advice regarding the development and placement of the important items. Moreover, the board itself should schedule matters of particular interest for future meetings; in this way, the president will have the opportunity to prepare information and draft proposed resolutions in an orderly manner and not under crisis conditions. Such reports will be assured of priority consideration.

The board is entitled to have all important questions of policy, irrespective of their controversial character, on its agenda.

Conduct of Business

Golden Gate University in San Francisco has a board of thirty-five trustees who meet once a month. The board consists primarily of representatives of San Francisco's business, industrial, and professional leadership (although two faculty and two student representatives are also included) and is interested in strictly business meetings. The board meets for a sandwich lunch and begins its deliberations shortly past noon. The chairman takes pride in adjourning at 1:30 on the dot, but a serious matter may continue the meeting until 1:45. The agenda and supporting documents are distributed a week in advance. Committees do a considerable amount of spade work, and their reports are complete, with clear written recommendations for action. Board discussion is brief and pointed but in good humor. The chairman expects to preside over a no-nonsense meeting.

The main campus of this institution consists of two downtown, almost adjacent buildings. The educational program is divided among three schools—law, business administration, and public administration—and there is a substantial graduate and extension program, mainly in military establishments. The student body, mostly career oriented, numbers close to five thousand, the majority attending in the evening. The institution is private and charges tuition, and although it has the usual administrative and development problems, it does not have to cope with many of the situations encountered on a large, diversified campus with a full daytime attendance, complex curriculum, more varied housekeeping questions, and extracurricular activities. Golden Gate runs a tight ship that could probably sail at near the same speed in heavier seas.

Most boards of public institutions, by contrast, whether single or multiple, will require one to two days, six or more times a year, to accomplish their business, partly because a fuller public discussion is expected. A sticky issue may be considered the first day and, with the benefit of evening discussions, be resolved the second— such as pending controversial legislation, or whether a downtown extension center should be established, or other educational policies related to innovation or expansion (which should be taken up *before* the pertinent physical facilities are considered).

The smaller the institution, the greater the tendency of the board to enter into administrative and fiscal detail. The time for the meeting should not be extended to accommodate this interest, but it should be sufficient for the board to satisfy itself that the mission of the institution is being carried out or should be changed or enlarged, that the administration is not oversized or overburdened, that financial requirements are being met, that education (the most important business of the institution) is being provided in a manner that appears to excite faculty and interest students, under the guidance of an administration alert to the needs and aspirations of both.

Open Meetings

One problem that haunts a public board more than a private board is the effect of its voting record. A public board performs in a glass bowl, conducting most discussions and taking actions in the public arena and before the press. Exceptions occur when the board considers personnel matters or pending litigation or, sometimes, the purchase or condemnation of land or facilities. (If owners or land speculators know in advance of the intentions of the trustees, they might take steps to make the purchase or condemnation more difficult and costly.) In California, the matter of secret sessions for all nonconstitutional boards is defined in statute and the areas of permitted secrecy circumscribed, as indicated in the exceptions just noted. The point is that most public business is conducted before the public, as it should be, and any attempt to evade the public-meeting requirement is usually strongly attacked by the press.

In any state where this kind of statutory requirement exists, it is important that the trustees bear in mind their public posture. Even where the statutory requirement is not binding but boards meet in public as a matter of policy, the same considerations obtain.

One consideration is whether the board appears to be an effective instrument of governance. Does it seem to know what it is doing? Does it seem to be informed about the problems and personnel of the institution? Does it give the impression of groping for solutions? More affirmatively, does the board show leadership, a willingness to grapple with issues, an understanding of the factors that underlie a policy determination, a dedication to the welfare of the university?

The board should recognize that most of its business is of public interest and should be conducted in public; its posture will improve if its members show that they have done their homework.

Agreement in Policy Making

Perhaps the best index of a board's effectiveness is its ability to procure near unanimity in determining policy, although unanimity is not a virtue in itself. A complex issue will have majority and minority viewpoints that may never be reconciled. Dissent among trustees may be a sign of conscientious and effective deliberations. But a board that is continually closely divided in its votes is in trouble. It may reflect a divided campus or aggravate an already existing division. Such a board cannot be sure of itself or convey a sense of solid judgment if its members struggle over a series of successive issues.

Questions of ROTC, admission policies, campus speakers, student newspapers, and censorship of campus theatre and art all may produce heated discussion and close votes. The board that is able to reconcile differences, to demonstrate cohesiveness and cooperation for the common good, will be better able to guide the institution than a board divided or bogged down in indecisiveness and repeated referrals to committee. The boards of private institutions may be less vulnerable, but only in degree rather than kind. In a crisis, the campus will know when the board is holding endless meetings and seems bewildered.

Although there must be differences, trustees are somehow expected to be able to reach agreement in most of their business. Reason is the cement of higher education, and governing boards should demonstrate their ability to find viable solutions through the exercise of reason. When trustees flounder on an issue, the fabric of the institution is weakened—reason seems to have failed. A similar situation occurs when the Supreme Court issues a series of five-to-four decisions with lengthy opinions and dissents. The people feel that a majority of one is not too convincing with respect to the rightness or justice of important social or political causes.

Unanimity in voting is neither essential nor desirable, but a constantly divided board will weaken the institution.

4

ESTABLISHING
DIRECTION

Generally, it is agreed that the board should establish the policies under which the institution is governed. It should not enter into the details of administration. It appoints the president or chancellor to handle administrative affairs and execute policy. But what is policy and what kinds of policy are the peculiar problems of the board? A policy usually settles a course of action or establishes a direction in some important matter. It is a regulation that may apply to any number of instances of the same nature; it does not attempt to isolate and deal with a particular instance unless the principle established would apply to instances of a similar nature.

Thus, matters of policy would be regulations on criteria for the admission of students, codes of conduct for students, conditions of tenure, and the establishment of a law or medical school. Policies need not be solely in the educational field; indeed, it has been reliably determined that only 15 percent of trustees' decisions are in this area. Many other decisions are more in the realm of management or important procedural regulation: determination of expansion, approval of architectural proposals, budgetary and financial recommendations or decisions. Rules governing institutional conduct are matters of policy. Yet the boundaries between policy and administration are not always clear. Policy declarations will sometimes set forth the procedure for implementation; it is well for trustees to be informed of such procedure, but it should not customarily be part of the policy declaration. In the words of President Lowell of Harvard College: "Laymen should not attempt to direct experts about the method of obtaining results, but only indicate the results to be obtained."

The first policy question that should confront the board member is the purpose of the institution itself. What are the goals of the college or university which he is supposed to implement? Unless he knows what his institution seeks to do, the subpolicies he develops may not be consistent with the objectives he was appointed or elected to carry out.

Each institution of higher education should have its goals, but it is almost impossible to orient an institution if the trustee does not have some conception of the general goals of all of higher education. Only with such knowledge will he know where his institution fails or how it should be modified or expanded.

Goals of Higher Education

It is odd that so little has been written of these goals. Occasionally, in a self-study such as recently occurred at the University of Oklahoma, a statement is attempted. Usually, the catalogues of our institutions of higher learning fractionalize the objectives and departmentalize the goals. Academicians become self-conscious when discussing their functions; objectives are stated in abstract and universal terms and are not helpful as guidelines. It may be that higher education is such a vast enterprise, its scope so wide and penetration so deep, so inclusive of every aspect of human thought and activity, that it may not be subject to articulation in any integrated statement. But since we are concerned with lay boards and their functions, it seems essential to provide some framework of reference for their work.

The term higher education itself may be uncertain or ambiguous. It is better to refer to it as education beyond the high school. In the United States it is governed by the principle that all persons should be given an educational opportunity to realize their potential, although it must be recognized that at any particular time this opportunity will be qualified by the availability of facilities and instructional services and by the needs of society.

With this idea in mind, I have tried to state eleven principal goals of education beyond the high school, culled from a number of sources and with some personal interpretation, and grouped according to some internal relationships:

(1) To give instruction in basic general education, mostly in the humanities, to develop the faculty of reason and the corollary faculties of objectivity, skepticism, and independent thought. It should inculcate a sense of history and an understanding of civilization, its complexity and interdependence, and the need for moral imperatives if civilization is to endure. It should cultivate the student's creativity and individuality; broaden the base of his intellectual, artistic, and recreational enjoyment; and help him understand himself and his relationship to society.

(2) To impart knowledge and skills in vocations and in specialized fields at the undergraduate level (such as engineering and nursing); and in the professions, old and new, at the graduate level (such as law, medicine, architecture, and social work). It should update the information and training of persons engaged in the practice of professions and vocations in industry, agriculture, business, and government.

(3) To develop new knowledge of every character, with priorities in areas of grave concern to the existing society, such as urban problems, health, and human survival, and also to make such knowledge available to aid society. It should engage in disciplined experiment in new areas and ideas and be innovative in improving teaching methods.

(4) To allocate available resources so that the needs of society will be met in the professions, industry, community services, and vocations, but avoid producing uneconomic surpluses in connection with filling such needs. It should make certain that the most able students will be challenged and the best leadership developed.

Other goals of education may be expressed more succinctly:

(5) To serve as critic of society and its institutions.

(6) To exercise affirmative effort to bring minorities previously suppressed into the mainstream of our educational, economic, and political life.

(7) To provide opportunities for remedial learning for those who have failed or dropped out along the way and for continuing education, irrespective of age, for career advancement and self-improvement.

(8) To afford opportunity for all persons to realize their potential on the basis of their abilities and diligence.

(9) To establish measures of progress and achievement.

(10) To help improve elementary and secondary education.

(11) To set a pattern of fair and effective governance (so that higher education partly demonstrates the worth of education by the way it conducts its complex relationships).

Within these general goals, particular systems and institutions must establish their own more limited goals.[1] For example, (1) the university will forego or give only peripheral attention to remedial learning; other institutions may emphasize it; (2) certain systems or institutions will forego expensive research institutes and professional schools; (3) certain institutions, including in-service training set up by industry, will stress the practical and the vocational; (4) certain institutions or specialized agencies will deal with continuing education both for the purposes of updating knowledge and for providing education for recreation and enjoyment; (5) private institutions may seek innovative methods and procedures not easily available to public institutions; (6) certain institutions will emphasize the training of competent teachers to instruct future generations of students.

In examining the outline of general goals, two points may be kept in mind. First, they concern both the individual and society. If these purposes are implemented, the individual has every opportunity to develop himself, to know what he is in the perspective of history and in the context of present problems; to cultivate his

---

[1] In a report on higher education (March 1971) to the U.S. Department of Health, Education and Welfare, a task force under Frank Newman, chairman, laments the homogenization of institutional missions and indicates that higher education would accomplish more for its students if it returned to a diversity of missions. In other words, all of our institutions should not seek to accomplish all the goals of higher education.

capacities for appreciation of the arts and of intellectual enjoyment; to understand and relate to his fellows in the college and in society. But society also has its claims upon higher education. It must obtain its leaders, managers, industrial and professional personnel, skilled farmers, and scientists from its colleges and universities. Thus, society will not permit higher education to concentrate its energies in a manner that will deny to society the personnel that it requires to continue its existence. If all students desire to become doctors, society cannot make funds available so that all can realize their ambitions. The individual's opportunity to realize his potential as a person pursuant to the goals of general education and related goals seems boundless. It is only in connection with professional and vocational skills that the law of supply and demand must operate in the primary interest of society.

Second, an outline of goals seems remote and somewhat irrelevant to day-to-day institutional operations. But actually if these goals were carefully observed and followed, they would have a profound influence on current academic issues. For instance, if reason were recognized as an essential criterion of university life, then mob action in defiance of reason would be seen as a betrayal of the institutional purpose. If an institution gives priority to the development of new knowledge as it may affect the most pressing questions in society, much concerning the problem of relevance is answered. If experiment in new areas must be undertaken in a disciplined manner, if a sense of history and an understanding of civilization are objectives of higher learning, then the character and substance of new curricula in ethnic studies will be guided into the most productive channels, particularly when related to the goal that minorities should be brought into the mainstream of our economic and political life. If a primary goal of higher education is to improve secondary and elementary education, then its own improvement is better assured.

Education beyond the high school has a number of goals, including imparting basic general education and professional and vocational training, developing new knowledge, and allocating educational resources so the needs of society will be met. It should also act as critic of society, work to bring minorities into the mainstream, provide remedial learning and continuing education, pro-

vide opportunity for all to realize their potential, establish measures of progress and achievement, help improve elementary and secondary education, and set a pattern of fair and effective governance. Generally, higher education should serve the individual in his own development and society in providing the leadership and professional and other personnel it needs to function. If all these goals were pursued, they would profoundly influence current academic issues.

Mission of the Institution

If the trustee is on the board of a university, then he must discover whether his university is an institution in the most complete sense—with high-cost professional and graduate schools, with the elaborate equipment of modern physics, with the curricula covering all the realms of knowledge. Such a trustee will have a different approach to the place of research in his institution than the trustee of a four-year college with a graduate school in two areas of study, even though, in accordance with American practice, it may be called a university. An institution in the midst of a city which has concentrated on supplying accountants and trainees for middle management personnel will be rather pragmatic (and probably negative) in terms of proposed extensive expansion into the liberal arts field.

The two-year junior college open to all high school graduates and providing for transfer to four-year institutions and for terminal vocational programs will have a more restricted educational mission. With its democratic admissions programs and its vital screening process, it is performing critically important functions in the area of higher education. Its counseling services at the base of the pyramid of education beyond the high school are of the utmost importance. The greatest mistake the institution may make is to attempt to convert into a four-year institution or to drop its vocational terminal programs. Thus, the trustee who is called upon to make decisions regarding the future of such an institution should do so knowing the function that it fulfills in the educational scheme and knowing its relationship to other segments of higher education.

The trustee of the private institution should be particularly conscious of his opportunity to authorize and support innovations which trustees of public institutions may not so easily determine.

The first consideration of the trustee is to know his own institution and the goals which pertain to it.

Almost every institution and system of institutions is reviewing its mission, and trustees should welcome the opportunities presented by such self-evaluation. The administration, faculty, and students can, along with trustees, participate in this project to ascertain and revitalize the purposes of the institution. Local advisory boards in a multiversity set-up can contribute at the campus level. This inquiry, conducted primarily by the constituent elements of the institution, can do more to restore a sense of academic community than any other endeavor. And the aggregate statewide results, even when adjusted to eliminate unnecessary duplications, should produce significant differences among, specializations in, and contributions from the institutions. Some will retain limited objectives in line with their specialized and historic contributions to the education of selected students; others will be more flexible in trying to adapt to our egalitarian era, which seeks to educate every person according to his potential.

But, in setting direction, even trustees in the most open institutions will take care before they confirm the modification or abandonment of prior standards. Too many times the argument for flexibility becomes an argument for no standards at all. There must be minimum standards of knowledge and competence in any discipline, profession, or vocation. Always there must be standards of excellence in relation to performance. The goal of more opportunity for more people to do more of their own things must not mean that educators find it acceptable that people perform on some mediocre level whatever they do. The direction must always be toward excellence; the requirements must be in line with the direction.

The trend to study and redefine missions indicates health and vigor in higher education.

Drawing upon the constituent elements of the institution, the board should establish its mission within the framework of the general goals of education beyond the high school.

5

POLICIES AND PRIORITIES

In achieving the goals outlined in Chapter 4, educational resources should be marshalled in a manner best calculated to eliminate needless duplication; to cause the young, in accordance with their capacities, to achieve at the accelerated pace required by modern life; and to utilize every avenue to give meaning to the educational process. Thus, the means for the attainment of goals may undergo constant reform. The lecture system, for instance, may be greatly curtailed in favor of library assignments and the use of tests and comprehensive examinations and essays. Or the level of performance required may be raised before a student is allowed to continue with upper division and graduate work. Or curricula may be reconstituted and new patterns developed for exchanging information and experience between the institution of higher learning and the surrounding community.

Delegation of Authority

Most boards of trustees have full legal powers of governance. However, it would be impossible for them to exercise their authority

40

on a day-to-day basis. Their legislative and administrative powers must be delegated. The chief executive officer (president or chancellor) is the recipient of most of the administrative delegation. In a multi-institutional arrangement, a further delegation may be to campus presidents or chancellors or to their governing boards.

Certain areas of decision, particularly the determination of curricula and the administration of faculty affairs, are usually given over to the organized faculty. Other areas of governance may be delegated to the students, such as the conduct of students activities, some student discipline, and the student union. Related to this delegation may be specific delegations of authority to the president to approve or veto the acts of the other segments.

Here we shall consider the specifics of some of the delegation problems, along with the trustee relationships to faculty, administration, and students. It is worth noting, however, that such delegations, once made, are usually hard to nullify or recover; they become hardened through practice and tradition, and they should not be lightly given or taken away. But there may be times of crisis or reorganization when it is necessary to recover, perhaps only temporarily, that which has been delegated. The delegated authority may have been misused or not have been exercised, or decentralization may have gone too far and resulted in irresponsibility or chaos. In any event, a board may be confronted with the hard choice of calling back a portion of its authority. Such an act is usually followed by great noise: it will be claimed that ancient rights have been flouted, that the board has become an enemy of democracy and autocratic, that it has no right in the premises. The wisdom and the purposes of the trustees' action may indeed be questionable, but the right of the board is usually crystal clear. If the board is indeed the agency responsible for governance; if the powers of governance flow from it, then unless contractually transferred or granted, the board has the right to recover such rights as it may have delegated. It may always be criticized for the manner in which it exercises its powers, but its right in law should be understood by all parties.

Delegations of authority to administration, faculty, and students must be deliberately and carefully made; such delegations may, on occasion, be recovered on a temporary or permanent basis, but it is a procedure fraught with friction.

Earned Degrees, Grading, Honorary Degrees

It is customary for the trustees to approve or grant all earned degrees upon recommendation of the faculty. This is the most perfunctory function that the trustees perform. In the absence of some unique case of fraud, the trustees must act upon the faculty recommendation that the student has fulfilled the course of instruction and is entitled to a degree. The participation of the trustees is to fulfill legal or ritual obligations.

The policy on grading has become a controversial issue. Many students contend that grading on an alphabetical or numerical scale interferes with learning and is merely a test for memory and regurgitation of the professor's lectures and views. A number of the faculty share their attitude and add that there are better ways of evaluation, if any should be applied. A few professors attempt to defeat the grading requirement by distributing A's and B's indiscriminately. The matter of grading seems to be primarily an issue for faculty who ultimately recommend the granting of the degree (an award that some also attack as restrictive and unnecessary).

But if grading is the established practice and it is not observed, should the trustees enter the argument? Most trustees appear convinced that grading is an essential though imperfect indication of achievement and of the student's right to continue to receive the benefits of a university or college education.[1] They concur with the more general academic opinion that examinations and other papers need not be exercises in repetition. Moreover, they agree that a no-grade policy would encourage the waste of much student time and be unfair to students wanting a record for employment, eligibility for scholarships, admission to graduate school, or personal evaluation. The institution itself requires such administrative aids.

Because trustees grant the degrees upon recommendation of faculty, they should not endorse a practice that may cheapen the degree, clothe it in ambiguity, or obstruct a needed administrative process. If adherence to the reasonable grading requirements of the institution is made part of the contract with a faculty member, the nonperformance or evasion of this condition can be an important

[1] A small university may be able to substitute teacher evaluations.

factor affecting reappointment, promotion, and tenure as recommended by faculty and approved by administration and trustees. (Such an overall policy could still allow for pass/fail or audit courses in areas of student interest where evaluation is not necessary to his academic program.) A dissident faculty member's protest that his academic freedom is being violated when he is cited for neglect or disregard of a reasonable grading policy seems far-fetched.

Honorary degrees may be a different matter. Boards of trustees usually reserve for themselves the right to select the grantees of honorary degrees, although recommendations are made by the president or chancellor and often the faculty participates. Some trustees will grant an honorary degree to any individual who gives the institution a sufficient amount of money. The exchange may not be contemporaneous, but one benefit soon follows the other. Some boards of trustees automatically award the commencement speaker with an honorary degree. Some boards grant prominent political figures an honorary degree, especially if they are in a position to help the institution secure needed public funds.

Other boards of trustees take a great deal of care in granting honorary degrees. They will always include faculty and scholars who have made notable contributions to letters and to science. They will include only those public figures whose life and contributions for the benefit of society should be an inspiration to youth. These boards are discriminating both qualitatively and quantitatively.

The image of the institution is reflected by the persons it honors. Honorary degrees that are "sold" for a consideration do not enhance the prestige of the institution and either become a joke or lower the status of the institution in the eyes of the community. The grant is purchased at too high a price. Others who may deserve this award of merit will refuse.

Some institutions, such as Stanford University, refuse to give any honorary degrees. This prohibition was written into the Stanford charter. Such a stand seems too prim and virtuous. There is a place in our national life for academic institutions to recognize outstanding merit and achievement for some common good through the granting of honorary degrees. They are not mere civilian decorations; they constitute the institution's award of a public honor. To be significant for the giver and the recipient, they must be based on considered judgment. Trustees should exercise that judgment.

Most trustees believe grading is an essential though imperfect indicator of achievement; they should not endorse a general no-grade policy, which may cheapen the earned degree. Trustees should award honorary degrees on the basis of merit and achievement; they should not be exchanged for gifts.

Campus Size

The matters of campus size and expansion are appropriately board policy. The board will decide this question partly on the basis of student demand and partly on the basis of funds available and to be counted upon for the future. In a public multiversity or multicollege system the board may not have complete jurisdiction to make the final decision; the legislature and the governor may have a decisive influence. But certainly the board should be in a position to carry its recommendations to the legislative body and to the public.

The board may consider that institutions beyond a certain size are too large for effective administration and tend to lose in academic quality. In 1948 the Strayer Report ("A Report of a Survey of the Needs of California in Higher Education") advised that urban state colleges in California should not exceed 6,000 full-time equivalent students; by 1960 the experts had raised this limit to 20,000 for state colleges and 27,500 for the university campuses. In other parts of the country student bodies have reached 35,000 to 40,000. Depending upon the circumstances of the growth of a particular institution and the kind of student population it serves, the governing board should be able to make a reasonable determination of a ceiling for student enrollment and then stick to its decision in order to protect the institution against deterioration. Lately, the figure of 20,000 has been given by the Carnegie Commission as the maximum size of a single institution. Near 10,000 may be the optimum size of a private university.

There seem to be four important questions to ask regarding campus size.

First, when is it more economically efficient to create a new campus than to expand an old one? This judgment should take into consideration the effective utilization of plant between 8:00 A.M. and 10:00 P.M.

Second, is sufficient space available so that there will not be undue congestion? What residence facilities for academic and non-academic personnel will be required, and will the housing and other necessary services be adequate? Will the larger institution disrupt the setting and ecology of the town and the surrounding area?

Third, what is the character of the campus and its programs? Are there many science and technical programs, which may require considerable laboratory space and not be able to handle as large an enrollment as humanities programs? Is it an urban campus whose students live in the community or is it a rural campus whose students must be housed, to a considerable extent, in dormitories?

Finally, what is the proposed organizational and academic structure of the institution? It should not be assumed that bigness requires depersonalization. It is possible to divide students into small groups and to provide the personal element. Allocating freshmen to cluster groups that share several classes together, providing a small college within a large university so that students can relate to their teachers and each other and study in a single dormitory-classroom complex with curriculum based on a unifying theme, using tutorials and seminars more and lectures less—all contribute to the human scale. A large campus is like a city; indeed it is a city. It can be lonely or exciting, and may offer a combination of group interests, freedom, and privacy that an independent small college cannot equal.

Higher education is faced with conflicting demands: on the one hand for mass education, which will increase size and impersonal, self-learning techniques, and on the other hand for humanization of the process. Most trustees are deeply concerned about personalizing contacts and emphasizing the faculty-student relationship; they should ask administration and faculty to develop the academic and physical structure—through class retreats, field trips, home visits, tutorials, and seminars—to provide the kind of personal element so that even if teacher-student contacts are fewer, they will be deeper and more significant.

Trustees should decide on campus size with these factors in mind: efficiency in operation, sufficiency of space, the character of the educational program, the human scale, and the nature of the community.

Admissions—General

The admissions policy will be related to facilities, educational mission, and campus size. California has a tripartite program for admissions: the ninety-six junior colleges are required to admit all high school graduates or their equivalent; the California State University and Colleges (formerly California State Colleges), nineteen operative campuses, draw from the upper one-third of the high school graduates; and the nine campuses of the University of California admit from the top one-eighth of high school graduates. Both of the senior segments accept transfer students with a C average who have completed their junior college requirements.

The result has been interesting. The State University campuses receive so many transfer students from the junior colleges that they have had to restrict the admissions of entering freshmen; the University of California campuses have been less successful in attracting the transfers[2] and are comparatively overweighted with entering freshmen. At a time of static or reduced enrollments, the University has discovered that there is a great deal of quality below the top one-eighth. The senior segments are willing to experiment in lowering admission requirements but not to the point of increasing the percentages of students who will permanently drop out because of academic failure. The junior colleges are better equipped to assist marginal students at less expense, though they are tuition free.

Some universities in the East have open access, but the tuition factor operates as a bar. Many universities in the Midwest have open access, but their failure rate is extremely high. The question of admissions must be dealt with on a statewide basis so that there is open access, buttressed by remedial assistance, and overall educational quality is preserved. When the number of eligible appli-

[2] Until the fall of 1973, the University of California required a 2.4 (C +) for transfers of those not eligible for admission to the University at the time of high school graduation. Fees at the University are $650 per annum compared with California State University fees of $180. These factors may have affected the volume of past transfers to the University.

cants exceeds the service capacity of the institution, then the board must procure additional financial support or it must restrict admissions on some equitable basis in order to preserve educational quality, with advance notice to the legislature.

The question of open access (disregarding high school grades and test performance) is usually determined by the legislative authority. Trustees will probably be asked their recommendations before such a policy is adopted and then will have to live with the decision. Since the question is of such profound importance to the future of our public educational policy, it calls for some further discussion and evaluation.

As noted, the midwestern universities have had open access for high school graduates for many years. The attrition rate has always been high. Thus, a somewhat dubious opportunity has been extended by the senior institutions. The largest scale urban experiment in open access is that of the City University of New York. In the two years since the policy has been initiated, enrollments have soared. CUNY has tried to allocate the marginal students to two of its institutions in order to concentrate assistance. Reports indicate that there has been a marked falling off in quality in many overcrowded classes throughout the university. No matter how strong the effort to implement the policy, there is great danger that the university will repeat the New York City high school experience. Students will either drop out (over one-third of those admitted have already done so) or transfer to studies with minimum requirements, and the bachelor's degree will lose much of its meaning.[3]

Admissions standards should be liberalized to accommodate legitimate demand, but suddenly to subject an entire system to open access seems unfair both to the students and to higher education. If standards are maintained, students will fail in large numbers. If standards fall, the general quality of education will fall with them, and the high schools will continue to pass their problems along to higher education. The more able or responsive students will not be challenged, will indeed be frustrated by the lowering of the common

[3] CUNY admits it may have lost in "polish" but replies that it has gained in service; moreover it is much too early to evaluate this great effort to answer New York City's needs.

denominator of achievement. The intellectual quality of the university's graduates will suffer.

The whole theory of complete open access at every level is based on some false notion of equal ability (instead of opportunity) and the idea that democracy requires a general leveling. Of course, as long as industry demands a university degree for many positions whether or not the duties require it, students will demand entrance to a university solely to obtain the degree. Industry must make realistic evaluations of job qualifications and not place an unwarranted premium on the university degree. If this principle were accepted, then the pressures for unrestricted access would be materially lessened.

The proponents for open access to all institutions of higher education contend that high school performance, university entrance examinations, and IQ ratings are not sound predictors of intellectual ability and that practically any student of sufficient age and with appropriate motivation can handle the university challenge. A further argument is that the university does not confer any benefits on bright students that they themselves do not earn, and the university's success would be better measured by the value it "adds" to those who enter the higher education race with cultural and intellectual handicaps. Certain of these contentions may be accepted, but to eliminate all selectivity is to repudiate public school education in the United States. Good high school performance has predicted fairly well the likelihood of success in the university. It may well be that the university program should be extended and greater effort made to answer the needs of various kinds of students and to tap previously unrecognized potentials, but not to the point where such a policy repudiates all prior intellectual qualification and achievement.

What is needed is that open access be guaranteed in at least one large part of the higher education system, along with suitable aids and assistance to motivate, encourage, and equip all students. If students succeed in the lower division of higher education, they should be able freely to transfer to other parts of the system for their further higher education. Moreover, in view of the imperfect nature of educational tests and unevenness in high school identification and motivation of certain students, the senior universities and colleges themselves should develop exceptions to admissions qualifications wherever they can establish the likelihood of the success of the student notwithstanding his lack of prior credentials. Pilot projects on a large scale should seek out such alternative qualifications. The senior institutions should broaden the scope of their admissions at least until the elementary and high schools catch up with their problems. In cases where the universities already provide open access, they should give substantive meaning to it through adequate financial aid and tutorial programs.

But public universities and colleges that have been selective may well continue such a policy (with exceptions as noted) in the interest of maintaining educational quality. There will always be gaps between the intellectual achievers at the university and those less able or willing to cope with the challenge. To reward the intellectual achievers with a competitive peer environment and accuse the process of being unfairly elitist is itself unfair. Granted that achievement can be measured partly by other than traditional devices, still the lowest passing denominator must not determine the level of all higher education. When the word *élite* was borrowed from French, it lost its accent; thus, our thrust should be to equalize opportunity so that anyone, through his effort and achievement, can become "elite."

Trustees are inclined to stress the maintenance of quality, and this position seems correct, provided that it is accompanied by a policy of liberalization of admissions (through exceptions) on a controlled basis and that complete open access be provided at least in the junior colleges.

Boards of higher education should have the right to set their admissions standards in order to carry out, within the scope of their appropriations, declared constitutional or legislative policy.

Admissions—Minority Students

One important group of students for a great many colleges and universities is the ethnic group. Actually, it consists principally of two large subgroups, the blacks and the third world, mainly Chicanos. These students were often militant in pressing their demands for higher education opportunity, but they did not participate with militant white students in their programs for social and political reform. They had and have two interests or demands: open access to higher education and development of ethnic departments and schools.

The black students were the original force in these matters. Their earliest demands (in the late sixties) were to break down admissions criteria entirely. Their argument was that they were kept from higher education because of white standards inapplicable to their experience. It was not fair to deny them a university education on the basis that the secondary school system had failed to motivate them about Victorian literature and the like.

Moreover, the upgrading of admissions standards to four-year colleges and universities after Sputnik had resulted in a lesser percentage of blacks qualifying for these institutions than before. California State University, San Francisco, was an example of the situation. The higher education master plan of California provided that, since 1960, state universities and colleges would draw from the upper third in achievement of the high school graduates. As a result, the San Francisco campus, which had enrolled from 9 percent to 12 percent of blacks before 1960, enrolled about 3 percent to 4 percent in 1968.

Blacks argued that their potential for doing creditable college work was as great as that of the white admittees but that the cultural racism embodied in elementary and secondary education prevented them from achieving and showing their potential. Therefore, they asked the colleges and universities to admit all blacks who were sufficiently motivated to come. And once in the institution, they asked for a special program of study that would be relevant to blacks alone. These were called black studies—black statistics, black political science, black psychology, and so on (see Chapter 7). They also demanded to administer the black curriculum. The students wanted to determine their own program of study, hire or approve the hiring of their own teachers, and operate as an autonomous department of study.

These twin demands for open admissions and independent black studies departments provoked sharp disagreements within the faculty and among administrators and trustees. All concerned recognized the necessity for making special adjustments in admissions in order to help make up for the past deficiencies in the public schools system. But to establish an enclave for unlimited free admissions, irrespective of qualification, threatened the entire program of higher education. Administrators imagined a situation in which an entire institution could be changed, its educational standards permanently diluted and its student body engulfed by such open admissions.

Actually, the black students and professors intended to recruit and screen on the basis of their own knowledge of potential in the black community. The slogan of open access was simply a technique to attract black students who otherwise feared the competition of the college. Their estimate was that the total increase of blacks in the student body would not go beyond 10 percent for some time. Yet, if adopted, the principles of such open admissions could well change the purpose and nature of the senior segments of higher education over the years.

This is a complicated subject involving the fears, aspirations, strategies, both long and short term, for a large part of the American population. But it is well to begin with two fundamentals. First, there are always a substantial number of black students who do as well as white students in their preparatory work, who compete on an equal basis, and who are fully qualified to enter American universities and colleges. They do so and they achieve. Usually they are the children of middle-class blacks who either themselves had attended public institutions of higher education or the established black colleges and universities of the South. Although they do not accept it wholly, these young people have adapted to a white-oriented educational program.

Second, there is the far greater number of blacks who come from the ghetto poor, who do not find books in their homes, who come from families who are relatively inarticulate, providing neither the facilities nor encouragement for study, or speak a language peculiar to the ghetto. These culturally deprived students have difficulty verbalizing and counting; they cannot read, write, or do arithmetic. To throw them into general and unqualified competition with white students would be manifestly unfair. The only way that they can be brought into a competitive position is to undergo training to remedy their cultural handicaps. They must learn to read, write, and count in college. It is idle to argue that they should have learned these skills in elementary and secondary school. They did not; they were passed along through their grades because of a sufficient amount of school attendance and because they grew older. It was the easiest way.

This is a hard but not unprecedented burden for higher education. Most colleges and universities for many years have had remedial English for freshmen. A great many white students who subsequently became quite successful have gone through the "bonehead English" course at the University of California. Sooner or later they had to learn to spell, to punctuate, to compose a passable sentence.

But the extent of the black students' deficiencies is much greater and the challenge much more difficult. The advantage is that many black students are highly motivated; they have been awakened and they are willing to work. These students with good potential should be provided for. It takes considerable financial assistance from Federal, state, and local grants. It takes patience and tutoring, but it can be done. Obviously, in the senior colleges and universities it should only be done with students who have such potential that they will be able, within a reasonable time, to do upper division and graduate work without such elaborate special assistance. The bulk of the remedial work should be performed by the junior colleges.

How long should this special assistance continue? Viewed in the light of the unhappy history of blacks in the United States, for so long as necessary. But it is quite obvious that the task is not fundamentally that of higher education. The duty to equip black students is in the public school system. I do not underestimate the public school problems in dealing with desegregation, with large classes and with noncooperative parents. Yet the basic preparation for higher education must be in lower education. Special large-scale efforts in remedial work for higher education should end in ten to twenty years.

But, as indicated, there must also be an end to special assistance within the educational process. If a student is not able to perform satisfactorily after two years of concentrated help, he should be transferred to some community program other than the upper division of higher education.[4] There is no use passing any student along simply to defer the moment of his ultimate frustration. On the consumer side, in the professions and semiprofessions the public must be served by those who have achieved their credentials.

Trustee policy toward the liberalization of admission policies for ethnic groups should recognize the necessity for exceptions to standard admission policies, financial and remedial tutorial aid to the disadvantaged, a cut-off point when the special admittee should be prepared for competition, the need to expand special efforts to locate and recruit minorities who do meet admission standards.

Tuition

One important factor in the educational-financial picture is tuition. Except for the junior colleges, the trend is toward the charging of tuition to students of public colleges and universities. The theory is twofold: first, tuition is a financial necessity to defray costs and, second, a student will be more appreciative or motivated if he pays for a share of his education. The first consideration is largely one of fact; the second is controversial, but since the first has been determinative for most public senior institutions, the board's problems deal primarily with the amount and use of the tuition money. The concern of most trustees is that the legislature will not increase funds to the extent necessary but will try to increase tuition (or compel the board to increase it) as a substitute for appropriations. To conserve tuition money, one great institution has limited use of the funds to scholarship and capital expenditures. By this device the operating budgets do not reflect the use of tuition.

This approach may be effective but is not logically sound. Tuition refers to the costs of instruction, to the student participating in the costs of his own education. The student should not be asked to help provide buildings for some future student generation nor should he be asked to pay the costs of other students through scholarships. The answer is made that the cost of instruction may

[4] Qualification: temporary assistance may be necessary to enable junior transfers and entrants to professional schools to make initial adjustments. Many disadvantaged whites also require special assistance.

well include a pro rate of depreciation or the "rental" of facilities, and that scholarship money merely merges in the total cost of the institution. But these arguments seem strained. It is better that the trustees should face the legislature with the direct challenge to provide adequate physical facilities for the educational program and to provide such scholarships as may be needed to ensure an equality of opportunity to students from low-income families.

In order to preserve educational opportunity for the whole population, the aim of the trustees should be to hold tuition to the minimum. This requires that trustees must be fully informed about state, Federal, and local resources. It means that they must be forever alert to protect equality of opportunity in higher education by taking public positions to hold down tuition charges on the one hand and to press for public scholarship funds on the other. The Carnegie Commission has recommended that tuition be held relatively low in junior colleges and the lower division of four-year public colleges and universities, but that students in the upper and graduate divisions eventually pay approximately one-third of instructional costs.[5] If scholarships were made available to assure equality of opportunity, there might be no objection. But adequate scholarship moneys always lag behind increases in tuition. Trustees, by seeking to keep tuition levels down throughout the institution, can use this leverage to procure appropriations for scholarships and liberal-term loans if tuition must be increased. However, there is also a question whether the upper-division and graduate students, generally the achievers most likely to repay society's investment, should bear a disproportionate tuition burden.

In order to preserve educational opportunity, the aim of trustees should be to hold tuition to the minimum. They should press the legislature to balance any necessary increases in tuition with adequate increases in scholarship and loan funds.

Research Policy

With the new emphasis on teaching, there is danger that research will be downgraded. A certain amount of research is

[5] *Higher Education: Who Pays? Who Benefits? Who Should Pay?* (New York: McGraw-Hill, 1973).

necessary to keep the teacher abreast of his field and is reflected in better teaching. Applied research—research directed toward some practical purposes—is important. It may improve the process of education itself or it may be directed to the improvement of some service to society. It is pure research—the research that may or may not have a practical effect and that seeks knowledge for its own sake—that has become suspect in terms of legislative appropriation. Yet a great university offering a variety of doctoral programs takes pride in the opportunity it affords to probe for new knowledge; to unveil the unknown; to reveal the past; to add to man's understanding of himself and his universe. The most distinguished universities in the Western world have supported this kind of research. In the interests of our cultural heritage, trustees must not permit this kind of research to be abandoned or greatly reduced, though it may mean contention with some executive and legislative bodies.

The board of a comprehensive university should vigorously defend the function of pure research.

Studies Abroad

At a time of financial stress for public higher education, the question may well arise as to the value of establishing, maintaining, or modifying an institution's study-abroad program. This program usually provides the opportunity for one, sometimes two, years of study in a foreign country, with continuing academic credit.

The prevailing pattern for public universities is to arrange with an institution abroad to admit and instruct a certain number of its students each year. A resident professor is sent along to assist the students, help coordinate courses and requirements, arrange for examinations and grades (most foreign institutions do not grade on an individual course basis), and act as counsellor and morale officer. Students are taught by instructors from the host country in the language of the country. They live in the regular student dormitories or in pensions. Facility in the foreign language is therefore a prerequisite; willingness to forego some amenities is frequently necessary. Overall costs should not exceed the charges that would otherwise be made for the same year of study at home. The American institution should be satisfied with the quality of the instruction before completing arrangements.

There are other kinds of study-abroad programs, some much more expensive. The American institution may establish a branch in the foreign country, transfer a part of its own instructional staff to operate it, and provide courses principally in the English language. This is institutionalized travel abroad; it has its comforts and its merits, but the less expensive procedure of attendance at the University of Madrid or Nice or Heidelberg or many others seems basically preferable and more productive of lasting results—for potential teachers of foreign language and literature, career foreign service officers, business representatives abroad, and simply those who desire to feel and live the life of another culture.

The fluctuation in value of the U.S. dollar will cause foreign study programs to be more expensive. This consideration, together with domestic stringencies, may prompt a review looking toward curtailment or termination. However, these programs should be regarded as having a high priority; for the most part they are restricted to highly motivated students seeking instruction relevant to their careers; they improve the conditions of international understanding; students speaking the foreign language make good ambassadors. A survey of the demands made upon students abroad and the quality and scope of their work is always in order, but proven programs should be continued and financial efforts stretched so that they can be. New ones should be established, to the extent feasible, where academic worth is approved.

By the same token, public universities and colleges in the United States should provide some reciprocal favorable treatment to foreign students here. One method of achieving this purpose is to hold down nonresident fees for such students and, in certain instances of hardship, to waive all or part of these fees, particularly for students from underdeveloped countries. Another aid could be in the form of scholarships, which the Federal Government mostly should provide, since the education of foreign students is considered to be beneficial to United States foreign policy. In any event, the presence of students from abroad, coming from different cultures, representing different values, is an enriching experience for American students and should be a continuing part of our educational scene.

Trustees should support study-abroad programs, particularly those in which students from their institution take instruction in a foreign university. They should also support programs for educating foreign students in their own institutions by granting a reasonable number of tuition waivers and scholarships, in whole or in part.

Defense Contracts

The question with respect to defense contracts, which has become a sensitive issue since the involvement in the Vietnam war, is whether a university that is publicly dedicated to the open cause of truth should contract to perform secret projects for the military. Apart from the political and moral question of whether higher education should be a direct resource of the military establishment, the issue does seem to turn on this question of secrecy. An institution dedicated to the spread of truth should not be involved in engaging in work that may not be revealed for decades. It is not a question of whether the work would ever be done. The Federal Government can establish or take over certain facilities; independent institutes can be established and experts can contract their services to such establishments and institutes. But it does seem to be in the best interests of higher education that it disengage itself from its military relationship. In doing so it will not only be consistent with its own principles but will also win the confidence of the young.

All of this is said with the knowledge that universities contributed heavily to the development of the hydrogen bomb and of gases and other agents of destruction during both world wars. It may still be a necessity for the government to require the use of university facilities during war time. But we have reached the point in international life when, as so many of our leaders have said, in a nuclear war there will only be losers, when war itself has become self-defeating as a matter of policy, when the overwhelming consideration is for survival and not for the preparation for a Pyrrhic victory. Thus, it should be the policy of boards of trustees to align themselves spiritually with the forces of survival. The contention that all university military research expenditures are for defense, not destruction, does not stand up in the light of recent history.

The board should seek to disengage from defense contracts (in peace time) involving secrecy.

Investments

Institutions with endowment or other reserve funds must keep them invested. Until recently the investment program of the university or college was strictly an economic affair, usually controlled by the prudent-man rule: trustees should keep the institutional funds invested in the way that a prudent man, carefully handling his own affairs, would keep his funds invested. Not many years ago, this was interpreted to mean government bonds and fixed-income obligations, but in recent years the university trust fund has been invested in stocks and other equities in much the same manner as a bank trust portfolio.

In the late sixties, students began to raise moral and political questions about the investment program, protesting investments in companies that did defense work or polluted the environment. The strict application of this principle could exclude a vast number of major corporations. The manufacturer of automobiles or of gasoline cannot claim that his product is free from causing pollution in varying degrees. A chemical company that devoted a bare fraction of its business to the production of chemical warfare products was a particular target of the students. Food-processing companies that did a vast defense business were usually disregarded. Sometimes steel companies were called into question; many times they were not, although they manufactured prime ingredients for defense hardware.

Implicit in this policy question concerning investments is a clash between economic and moral values. A literal compliance with student demands would have a grave effect on the ability of the trustees to make prudent investments in the accepted sense. But trustees can and probably should heed or anticipate a protest against investing in a company that, let us assume, is producing atomic warheads or a company against which the government has filed serious pollution charges related to continuing practices. At some clear point higher education that assumes a high moral posture must recognize the moral claims of its students, even though their relationship to the investment portfolio may seem remote.

In a much broader sense the moral dimension has a special hold on trustees. Most boards have reluctantly come to the conclusion that their institution does not stand in loco parentis to the students, but the tradition lingers that the college or university should have a positive influence or attitude toward moral values and that the students should be aware of them. Trustees cannot impose a moral code on student behavior, but they can, through the exercise of their policy-making power, help administration and faculty to provide conditions on campus that will encourage civility, self-respect, social responsibility, and mutual consideration.

The board should consider moral and social values of importance to students in determining its investment portfolio.

Rights and Responsibilities

As the governing body of the institution, the board of trustees should establish or approve policies and procedures that ensure the members of the academic and student communities of their rights and responsibilities. Students should have the right to elect a substantial part of their courses, to assemble, to speak their minds, to hear off-campus speakers, to live their private lives, and generally to act in a manner that does not injure others. At the same time they should have responsibilities—to refrain from violence and acts that injure others, to respect the rights of fellow students, to listen to both sides of an argument at a campus meeting without disrupting either speech, to write their own papers and examinations. The consequences of the breach of responsibilities should be known and so should the procedure of discipline for establishing these consequences, and other students should share in hearing and administering the discipline. All students should have a brochure outlining the benefits and conditions of their academic citizenship.

Similarly, faculty should have a charter of their freedoms and responsibilities and the procedure for administering the consequences of breaching them. A board should require that the appointments and the conditions for appointments for faculty should

be in writing and thus the professor's contractual rights and obligations made known to him. These matters will be considered later in
more detail, but here it is pertinent to note the importance of such
declarations as a matter of policy.

*The academic and student communities should have a clear
statement of their rights and responsibilities.*

Change of Name

The question of change of name—from *college* to *university*
—arises with increasing frequency as public four-year colleges aspire
for prestige. The answer rests partly on what is meant by the word
university. Since it originally meant corporation, not much help is
derived from the origin of the word. Moreover, the earliest users of
the name were not comprehensive research institutions, but "corporations" often limited to the training for a single profession such as
law or medicine. The idea that a university must be a more diversified institution, with an extensive graduate and research program, is
more of a nineteenth-century development. At present, perhaps half
of America's universities, do not offer the doctorate.

Actually, the word college carries with it most of the traditional academic values. The various colleges of Oxford and Cambridge are central to those universities and constitute the strongest
ties of allegiance and pride. Harvard College and Darthmouth College remain great names. But many in academic life and most laymen attach great importance to the name university as opposed to
college, because the term college has been used by vocational schools
for barbers, secretaries, cosmeticians, and morticians. Therefore,
institutions of higher education seek the university label on grounds
of status, and presumed appeal for faculty recruitment, student
enrollment, and legislative appropriation. If the term college does
not have its own particular significance for an institution, there is
much precedent in the current American practice for trustees to
change the name of their institution to university or, if necessary, to
request legislation or other authorization for the change of name.
The change will not accomplish any miracles, but it may indicate
that the institution is keeping up with fashion. Eventually, when

funds are easier to procure, the change may stimulate expansion into graduate or research programs (for good or ill).

One aspect of the name change should be watched—namely, the effects, if any, on regional accreditation. Normally, a change in name without a change in function will not adversely affect accreditation, but it is well to check the matter in advance.

A change of name from college to university may add a measure of prestige but will not accomplish miracles. It also may stimulate efforts to expand into graduate or research programs.

Intangibles

Much has been made of the need for moral purpose in education. Trustees should not be hesitant to declare that there are such moral imperatives to be achieved in part through higher education's service to the community and in part through aiding the student's self-development.

An important moral issue for the student rises directly out of the scientific and technological developments of this era. It is abundantly clear that knowledge can be power for good or ill; it can build or destroy, cure or inflict pain, make life comfortable or unbearable. Higher education must demand that knowledge is power to be used responsibly, that the end does not justify the means inside or outside of the academy.

The moral element of education is a charge to faculty. Trustees and the president can and should espouse it, but faculty must implement it.

On a related plane is the matter of satisfying personal needs. Students are concerned to avoid a treadmill of work, mere accumulation of goods, and superficial pleasures. They want to be able to cope with their expectations of leisure. Trustees should give policy and budget support to the liberal arts and humanities—which until recently had lost the luster of relevance—as the subject matter most pertinent to self-development and the rich fulfillment of a good part of leisure time.

6

PRESIDENT AND ADMINISTRATION

It has frequently been said that the most important single function of any board of trustees is the appointment of its chief executive officer—the chancellor or president. This official is the one the board will have to rely on to carry out its policies. He will in many ways become the image of the institution. Hopefully, he will provide leadership to the faculty and inspiration and motivation to the students.

Selection of President

Usually, the selection process begins with the appointment of a selection committee. It is most important that this committee be representative of institutional interests other than the trustees, as well as of the board itself. A rainbow committee, drawn from different segments of the college community, chaired by a trustee but including substantial faculty and some student representation, may be the best answer. In a multi-institutional system, it would be well if the presidents of one or two of the institutions were also included. Because the new president or chancellor will be the executive officer

62

of the board, trustees should constitute the majority of the selection committee, although a majority made up of board members and administrative members (in the multi-institutional situation) may be feasible. A typical committee set up may include (1) four trustees, two faculty,[1] and a student;[2] or (2) five trustees, two faculty, and two students; or (3) four trustees, a college president from within the system, two or three faculty, and one or two students.

The involvement of faculty and students in the early stages of the selection process is important because the head of the institution should be called to his office by its major elements and should be acceptable to them. Otherwise, he may be defeated from the beginning. One reason the average college president lasts only five years or less is that the principal groups making up the institution were not asked to participate in the choice.

On an operations basis, it does not seem to matter how a committee is made up; in most major institutions the selection procedure appears to be the same. The committee meets and decides that it will obtain the names of one hundred of the greatest academic leaders in America. They will request names from the great foundations such as Carnegie or Ford; from national associations of universities and colleges; from the faculty leadership and individual faculty members; from the alumni and student associations; and from others, including, of course, the committee members. The current presidents of Harvard or Yale are usually on the list, and the sky is the limit for candidates.

Biographies are obtained and the list shakes down. Certain candidates are obviously too old, a few may be too young, a substantial number will be unavailable.

The aim, of course, is to secure the very best candidate who

[1] Faculty probably should be excluded if the institution bargains with a faculty union. (See also Chapter Ten). Many trustees and observers believe it is a mistake to include faculty under any conditions (because they are "employees" and the president is "management"). But in most institutions where the functions of governance are traditionally shared, the significant participation of faculty in the selection process is the most sensible course.

[2] Many boards will not accept students on the committee, yet the president should be a person to inspire students. Student reactions to a candidate can be most valuable.

will have the qualifications of an outstanding administrator, a brilliant research scholar who is well respected for his academic achievements, a man who commands the respect and cooperation of faculty, a bridger of the generation gap who can persuade and influence the young, an astute strategist who can avoid or dissolve student confrontations, an executive who can influence the business community and procure development funds even for the public university, and a charmer and beguiler of the alumni. And if he is to be the head of a public institution, he must be a leader who can make friends with legislators, impress the governor, and obtain the necessary appropriations. All of these accomplishments he should be able to perform with a lively and entertaining sense of humor.

It will not be long before the committee recognizes that this superman does not exist and that they will have to settle for less. The list must be pruned several times, occasionally a name added, and finally a small group of possibilities will be presented.

In the course of these investigations the comments of the executives of the national foundations and academic and professional associations will be most valuable. Because they deal with the institutions throughout the country, they know of the migration of presidents from place to place, the problems they have encountered, the victories won, the defeats sustained. When the choice is actually narrowed, the most helpful advice is that given by some trusted administrative officer or faculty member who has been able to view closely the candidate's performance from within an institution he has served. But a candidate's printed addresses to students or faculty and his commencement addresses should not be overlooked since they give a clue to his style and reach.

When the list reaches six or seven names, interviews in depth are in order and a staff member should be sent to check references, reputation, and performance on the spot (the most polished interviewee may turn out to be on the run from his creditors). It is better that the candidate be brought quietly to some neutral place in the community for the interview in order that his interest in the position be kept confidential and that his own position in his current institution be protected.

Direct contacts by committee members with their friends

on other campuses should be sparingly used. The situation easily can get out of hand. Channeling committee inquiries through experienced, trusted staff investigators should produce the best results. Occasionally, however, where there is a close relationship between a committee member and the source, and the source is potentially important, direct contact should be permitted.

Leakages of information regarding candidates, especially when reported in the press, can be most embarrassing. Committee members should be made aware, in the strongest terms, of their confidential trust. Overlong searches increase the possibility of leakages and the risk of losing desirable candidates.

Finally, the selection committee will make its recommendation to the entire board, and the board would do well, in executive session, to speak directly to the two or possibly three leading candidates. The board should make its decision but defer the announcement, of course, until after the successful candidate has advised the authorities whom he has been serving. In practically all instances his current board will be understanding and cooperative; no management wishes to hold a man after he has determined to leave. In some instances, there may be a last-minute effort to persuade him to remain by financial inducement or otherwise, but an agreement made with the type of executive the board wants will stick.

The selection procedure just discussed is not fixed or standard. It is not essential to begin with the one hundred "best" names. If sufficient preliminary inquiry is made, ten will usually do. But somehow most selection committees seem to feel that unless they mine every vein they will not find the gold they seek.

Not every institution can seek a sixty-thousand-dollar president. Smaller institutions would do well to ascertain the names of the executive vice-presidents or academic deans of similar institutions. The young, vigorous administrator who has begun to make his mark, who has had a measure of experience but has not yet held a top post, may be just the leader you want. The man *raised* to a president may be the better man.

The board should be concerned that the candidate does not seek the office as a stepping-stone to a better job or to use the interview process as a way of bargaining for a higher salary or promotion in the institution he is currently serving in. However, the board should not necessarily reject a young, ambitious, able man just because he will probably outgrow the institution in a few years and at such time will quite likely transfer to a larger or more prestigious institution. The potential of a sizable interim contribution in the post for which he is being examined may justify the appointment.

The board will wish to check a candidate's record: how he related to faculty (organizations and individuals) and students; whether he had any problems with his board (and, if so, whether it was a clash of personalities, a substantive issue in which the board or the candidate appeared to be in the wrong, or a significant disagreement over principle); what kind of deputies he selected; what judgments he was compelled to make under trying conditions; what his philosophy of administration was (whether he makes decisions with or without consultation, or by consensus, or does not decide at all). Committee information should provide the answers or leads to most of these questions.

Finally, in the presidential search, trustees should not overlook the president's wife. She might be able to contribute greatly to the welfare of the institution as its first lady, or she might be a serious handicap. While the president's personal affairs are his own, they do spill over to make his official life easier or more difficult. If they often indicate problems, the appointment may not be worth the risk.

The possibility of a woman president should not be overlooked. This prospect will increase as women gain more experience in presidencies of coeducational institutions and in deanships and vice-presidencies. In due course, the husband may be the secondary problem!

One point to be kept in mind: the board may decide to reject all recommended candidates and continue the process of search.

The committee to recommend upon the appointment of the President is perhaps the most important board committee; it should include nonboard members from administration, faculty, and students. It should not base its interviews on too long a list or dream impossible dreams.

The president's qualifications should include: academic stature; administrative experience; ability to relate to faculty, stu-

dents, and government officials; ability to cooperate with the Board; a spouse who will be of help in these relationships.

President's Contract

It is, of course, important to have a clear, mutual understanding of rights and responsibilities. The salary must be specified together with any fringe benefits. If a home goes with the position, it should be so stated. If it is thought that a home may be made available in the future, it should be understood whether this idea is a hope or a promise; if it is the former, it should be agreed that the failure to produce it will have no effect on the arrangement.

If pension rights are not transferable, this fact should be known and accepted by both parties. In a major appointment in higher education in California, the chancellor so appointed misunderstood or did not know that his pension benefits were not transferable from another state. The possible loss of the hard-earned and very substantive pension rights he had accumulated was the principal cause of his leaving the new post within a year.

A contract term is usually not stipulated. It is better for the institution and for its leader to have freedom in this respect. If the chief executive loses control of the institution, or if he finds that he is unable to work with the board, an unexpired contract period will only be an obstacle to the inevitable and necessary dissolution. The attitude of most Presidents is, if they don't want me, I no longer want them.

The president's contract should be clear as to rights and perquisites, and he should serve without any fixed term.

Role of President

The principal working relationship for trustees is with the president (or chancellor) and his staff. Most of effective governance depends upon the success of this relationship.

The trustees, presumably after great care, have selected their administrative head. But he is a unique leader: a professional in academic life, the executive of an administrative bureaucracy, and the representative of the institution to the public and to the governmental structure. He is not a mere employee of the board. Normally, in recognition of his stature, he is a member of the board, ex officio, during the period of his incumbency.

The president should represent the faculty position to the board, even if he does not concur in it and says so, and notwithstanding that the official faculty body has its own officers who may present a faculty viewpoint independently. His role is to bring unified leadership to the institution.

This view of the president's status and functions is not universal. Former University of California president Clark Kerr has described the president's roles in a multiversity as being "mostly a mediator." [3] His first task, Kerr says, is "peace within the student body, the faculty, the trustees; and peace between and among them." His second task is "progress," in which he becomes the "central mediator among the values of the past, the prospects for the future and the realities of the present." The effective mediator must, at times, "sacrifice peace to progress," Kerr believes, as when "needed innovations . . . take precedence over the conservatism of the institution." A president obtains this when he achieves an accommodation between the centers of power within and outside the institution, and moves "the whole enterprise another foot ahead in what often seems an unequal race with history." Others have remarked on the president of a public university as a conciliator, an achiever of consensus among disputing factions, a super-adjuster of pressures from trustees, faculty, students, alumni, the legislature, and the governor.

Unquestionably, the president of a great institution of higher education, with many branches and an astronomical budget, must take into consideration a variety of interests before exercising his judgment. To survive, he cannot be too far removed from trustees, or from faculty and student concerns, in administrative action or in recommending policy. But he is chosen to be a leader and he should lead. Whenever possible he should establish the consensus, but there are times when he must decide irrespective of consensus.

The board of trustees should receive recommendations from the president with a presumption in favor of their validity. Analysis and discussion may change their viewpoints and bring about adjust-

---

[3] Dr. Kerr leads quite effectively while he mediates.

ments from both sides or perhaps a refusal to approve, but the point of departure should be one of confidence.

The president no longer speaks from the lofty pedestal of a nineteenth-century educational dictator, but he still wears the robes of high authority and still has the opportunity to know more about his institution than anyone else. Thus, if he retains a clear view of educational purposes and speaks to his trustees persuasively and with candor, giving them the facts and keeping them abreast of his thinking, he has more than a fighting chance to succeed. In times of trouble, his most important challenge may be to conserve the university or it may be to effect changes that the changing society requires. The *initiative* belongs to him.

This does not mean that the board should be a rubber stamp for presidential statements or that all votes should be close to unanimous. There are times when the president must take a stand for educational values or for budget requests even though opposed by members of the board, including powerful political officials. But the board should endeavor to support its president most of the time and the president should not attempt to draw issues unnecessarily in situations where he knows the vote will go against him. If philosophical or other differences reach the point where a decent working relationship becomes impossible, then resignation or removal may be the only solution.

In a constructive working relationship, problems are usually solved in the committee stage when vice-presidents, specialists in their fields, initially propose policies. The president does not have a stake in every policy and will carefully select those he feels he must press.

The president will attend the committee hearings dealing with the most important issues. Vice-presidents will represent him at other committee hearings. The procedure at all these meetings should be much the same. Trustees should be as diligent in asking questions and testing assumptions as they need to be, but this rarely calls for the tone or procedure of hostile cross-examination. The object of the committee (or board) hearing is to develop policy, not to seek out personal deficiencies. If incompetence is exposed, it should be reported to the president.

The president has the responsibility for keeping the board

informed. This means, in addition to his oral reports, the supplying of background materials supporting the agenda items. It also means calling the attention of the trustees to important articles, speeches, essays, and developments in the field of higher education which will assist them in determining board policies. The temptation of the administration is to bury the trustee under a mass of mineographed materials and let him dig his way out. The better way is to summarize the most pertinent information and to provide the surveys and reports to which the summaries relate as references. The homework required of a trustee is to understand the problem and the proposed policy, not to evaluate dissertations.

General articles and critical reviews may be distributed at any time. They should be selected with care and pertinent passages should be marked. Administrators are fairly conscientious about their attempts to keep trustees informed; the most frequent complaint of the trustee is that he is inundated and will be compelled to build an addition to his house for filing his materials. Most spouses of trustees will provide an easy solution to the disposition of materials over a year old that are not indexed: throw them away. You will never locate what you have haphazardly stored.

In view of the tons of materials furnished to trustees, much of which is read, it seems unfair to accuse them of being illiterate about higher education matters, but this comment is frequently made. The truth seems to be that trustees read a great deal about higher education problems, but not in an orderly way. In addition to reading whatever materials are given them by the administration, trustees should try to include the following: (1) the four-page *EPE 15-Minute Report for College and University Trustees,* published by Editorial Project for Education, Inc., Washington, D.C.; (2) the eight-page *Chronicle of Higher Education,* published weekly during the academic year; (3) *AGB Reports,* a periodic publication for members of the Association of Governing Boards of Universities and Colleges; and (4) regularly one of the provocative periodicals dealing with education matters such as *Change.* Reference to a faculty periodical such as the quarterly *AAUP Bulletin,* published by the American Association of University Professors, is also very much in order.

The attitude of the trustees to the operation of the administrative hierarchy is of considerable importance. If the trustees of, say, a statewide college system regard themselves as a governing board handing down orders to a chancellor, who then deals through his vice-chancellors with the campus president, who orders his own vice-presidents to direct their deans to instruct the department heads to order their faculty to deal with their students—it will not work. The university does have business aspects and it does have a hierarchy, but it is not a business and cannot be operated as a business or as a typical government agency. There are too many professionals involved in the process, too many persons who must exercise initiative and judgment almost as though they were self-employed. And the person who ordinarily would be at the base of the pyramid is not an ordinary worker in the vineyard; he is the professor, the teacher, the researcher at the very center of the process. The governance of a university requires a pooling and sharing of specialties. Important recommendations on educational policy should come from the professors in charge of the classrooms. Communications must run in both directions. Ultimately, policy decisions must be made and become operative all the way down or across the line. But the process of decision making may commence at any level.

The president should be a leader, not merely a mediator or consensus taker, but he cannot be expected to operate the institution as a business. The president must keep the board informed, and the trustee must do his homework.

Relationship with President

This position of support of the chief executive should continue during his incumbency. There may be differences of opinion —the evaluation of his recommendation is always in order—but the general posture should be one of support as long as the board desires that president. Taking issue with the president at an open meeting, criticizing him or repudiating his program in a confrontation may end his usefulness to the board and to the institution. If a personnel issue develops between the president and the board, it should be handled initially by the chairman of the board, an ad hoc committee, or, perhaps, the board in executive session. A board cannot

publicly and continuously negate a president's recommendations without endangering the relationship and the effectiveness of the presidential office. If issues have to be drawn, they must be, but with the knowledge of the consequences.

The chief executive officer is entitled to appoint his vice-presidents, subject to the approval of the board. If he desires changes in the top echelon, he should be permitted to make them. He will be held accountable and responsible to the board, and he should be permitted to surround himself with administrators who will command his respect and confidence. Often, the faculty will wish to have a voice in these appointments. In connection with certain offices, such as the academic vice-president, the president would do well to consult the faculty leadership. But although he should consider their interest and views in making such an appointment, he should not appoint a deputy in whom he lacks full confidence. In other words, he must not accept someone else's agent.

Actually, the time may come when the board considers that it must take administrative action in order to preserve the institution, irrespective of the president's status. For example, the institution may be in such an exposed and difficult position that the board cannot wait to fire the president and replace him; perhaps under prevailing campus conditions no qualified person could be induced to take over a weakened and confused institution.

Consider two examples. The college art department has sponsored an exhibit that includes a number of pictures on sexual subjects, which may offend some students and many of their parents, and a newspaper article has characterized the exhibit as dubious art and in poor taste. The president has investigated the matter and has decided that although there are offensive features, the art faculty has found the exhibit to be artistically and culturally justified. He does not approve it, but he recognizes that it is scheduled for only three more days and considers that it is better to permit it to continue than to try to censor it and close it down in whole or in part. Members of the board have read the newspaper criticism and have been contacted by some irate citizens. The board receives the report from the president setting forth his views and reasons for inaction. The board resolves that the art exhibit shall be closed forthwith and directs the president to carry out its order.

In this situation it does not appear that the existence of the institution is threatened, though it had been subject to some bad publicity. The president may have disregarded certain options that were open to him in dealing with the faculty and in failing to bring about some kind of satisfactory adjustment. Freedom of communication, matters of tactics, questions of judgment were certainly involved. But, apart from any other considerations, the board probably committed an error in overruling its president if it desires to preserve his leadership. He cannot stand many incidents of this kind of direct action from the board and still do an effective job.

On the other hand, suppose the institution is in the throes of a series of violent demonstrations. The president and the faculty have been unable to control the situation, and the students have occupied two of the principal buildings. Violent assault has injured a number of students. The president has pleaded with the students in vain and, indeed, while hostage in his own office has conceded to certain extreme demands regarding the retention of faculty members who, he has previously told the board, are thoroughly unqualified; and he is reported to be on the verge of agreeing to the establishment of a department whose dean and professors will be student-approved or appointed. The president is tired and confused, though he wants to be cooperative. No other executive of sufficient stature seems to be available to become acting president, and in any event immediate removal of the president might cause the entire campus to explode in a riot. The board, by resolution, repudiates any agreements made and withdraws authority from the president to make any other agreements. It directs the president and each of the vice-presidents to request the police to come on campus to restore order, and it appoints a committee of the trustees to deal with the student demands and report back to the board as in their judgment may be necessary. In this case, the safety of the campus and students are at stake; there is a vacuum in authority, and the board enters into administration in order to preserve the institution. To state the problem and the action taken is not to contend that the matter is solved, only that the board is justified in taking direct action.

The general posture of the board must be one of support as long as the board desires that the president remain. The board may act administratively in an emergency when there is a vacuum of administrative authority.

7

WORKING WITH FACULTY

Perhaps the most sensitive relationship that exists in an institution of higher learning is that of the board of trustees to the faculty. Much depends on the attitude of the board and the understanding and approach of each board member to faculty status.

In most colleges and universities, the board that considers the faculty to be mere employees may have a difficult time governing the institution. The member of the faculty, of course, considers himself as a member of an ancient and dignified profession and expects to be treated accordingly.

The faculty and the student mix determine the quality of the institution, but the faculty is the decisive element in the quality of the education. The board must accept this premise. The faculty is the continuing part of the institution and ultimately will spell its success or failure. The board, therefore, should seek, through the administration and otherwise, to cooperate with faculty. The board should endeavor to establish procedures that will facilitate a constructive relationship between faculty, administration, and students. A board at war with its faculty is fighting the institution itself.

Understanding the Faculty

In view of the importance of faculty to the institution, the board should be greatly interested in the program of faculty recruitment and in the operation of the tenure system. This means that the board should be satisfied that the policies controlling recruitment and tenure are designed to procure and maintain a faculty of high caliber.

All of this may sound obvious and like a pious platitude, but too often the trustee attitude toward faculty is negative rather than positive. This results partly from the attitude and conduct of many faculty members themselves. Faculty consider themselves as "we" and the administration and the trustees as "they." It does not matter that one of their own number may become a dean, vice-president, or president. As soon as he leaves the faculty, even temporarily, during the period of his administrative office, he is "they"; he has metamorphosed from Dr. Jekyll into Mr. Hyde. Sooner or later the board senses this hostility to administration and governance and begins to feel as though it is part of "they."

Part of this polarization is due to the fact that faculty consider that board administration and trustees are invaders of territory that orginally belonged to them. In the days of the medieval universities and still today in the colleges of Oxford and Cambridge, the faculty constitute a major part of administration; they select the heads of their scholastic communities.[1] The faculty may grudgingly admit that the size and complexity of most American campuses require an administrative staff and possibly a board to take care of the household chores of the institution and perhaps certain external affairs. But they would prefer that the administration maintain the plant and leave the operations to them.

This attitude may be quite erroneous, for even the oldest of the English universities have found that more and more the admini-

---

[1] Faculties are also heavily represented in the Councils, which are are a part of the governance of the comprehensive British universities.

strative function requires separate personnel and expertise, that a faculty cannot administer the institution on off hours. But a board of trustees should recognize that the proud feeling that "we" are the university or the college is a fact of life with which they must cope in the handling of faculty relationships.

Moreover, university and college teaching constitutes a unique profession. It is highly individualistic; the most important part of the work, whether it be teaching or research, is performed away from any kind of direct supervision. The professor is an authority figure to the students. He gives his lectures and conducts his courses and examinations pretty much in his own way. He has an area of specialization which he is inclined to regard as his intellectual territorial preserve in his institution.

Particularly in the liberal arts, words are his life. He describes with them, he investigates with them, he contends and argues with them. Of course, we are all creatures of words, but not in the same way as the teaching profession. A professor espousing a certain theory of economics or political science or history can lock himself into a bitter struggle with four or five colleagues around the world and consider himself quite seriously to be defending against the barbarians at the frontiers of knowledge. Thus, if he also comes into disagreement with the administration and trustees about some matter close to his interest, he may speak or write with similar vehemence and perhaps outrage.

If he is to deal sympathetically and constructively with faculty, the trustee must understand that (a) faculty interest in governance derives in part from tradition and (b) individuality and even loneliness are inherent in the academic life.

Curricular Decisions

There are times when the board comes close to making curricula determinations—namely, when it approves the college or university budget. If funds are limited, as in the case in most institutions today, certain programs will have to be deleted or restricted. But in most instances the problem must be referred back to the administration and the faculty. A lesser sum may be allocated for letters and science or for the education of elementary and secondary teachers, but deciding which particular departments or courses are to be cut should be the responsibility of academicians, who are best qualified to weigh the priorities.

This would not apply to the elimination of an entire school. If it should be ascertained that the law school was a losing proposition, that it had lost accreditation, that its students were not passing the bar examination in any competitive percentage, and that other institutions were serving the need in this area of professional training, it might well be indicated that the board should terminate the operations of the law school. Similarly, if the demand for an engineering school had fallen steadily over a period of years and it was clear that other institutions were more attractive or had taken up the slack, the board might well determine to suspend or end the life of the engineering program. Of course, these decisions will affect curricula; indeed, almost any large budgetary decision will do so. But the board should be dealing with the type of decision that relates some segment of the curricula to an educational goal and not to the contents of a course.

In a rare instance, an exception may arise, as when a course is given which appears directly contrary to the purposes of the institution or which, in the opinion of the board, seriously compromises the purposes or the image of the institution. This kind of situation may arise in the innovative programs. Recently, in order to meet student demands for relevance, permission has been given to establish courses on a credit or noncredit basis which have little traditional background and which are decidedly experimental. Student leaders or groups may have been given latitude in the development of such courses by a faculty sponsor who has approved the general outline. But then, it may turn out, the students are studying methods of guerrilla warfare and urban revolution or they are involved in some sex education course which, at least descriptively, suggests that the experimentation may be more than academic. The board should be slow to take action; investigation may show that the class has been promoted by an extravagant label but that the content is within acceptable limits. Students will soon drift away from a pretentious noncredit course that has little to deliver. The board should listen carefully to the recommendations of administrators, faculty, and students and any actions proposed at these levels. Only as a last resort should the trustees take direct action, even in a case that appears to be a flagrant violation of educational principles.

Trustee prohibition of any course or course credit will produce anguished cries about the invasion of academic freedom. No self-respecting faculty wishes to be identified with a nonsense course, and it may be the better part of wisdom to permit the faculty to handle the matter of termination, even if it must continue a dubious offering to its scheduled end.

The board should not deal with individual course content but should be concerned with the standards and procedures under which a course is added or deleted.

ROTC

Another curricular issue that may return in the seventies to be determined by the board is the presence of ROTC on campus. Many institutions withdrew their programs in the last decade under student and faculty pressure; the marching ROTC was a symbol of the draft and the hated war. With the termination of hostilities and the conversion to a volunteer army, the issue may again be presented whether students who wish to prepare to enter a volunteer army should be given the opportunity to do so on college campuses.

It is difficult to justify the right of some students, even a majority, to prevent other students from preparing for a career that they wish to pursue—a lawful and honorable career supported by national policy and appropriation. Why should such preparation be prohibited, while preparation for other government services be permitted? The view of faculty, discovered after almost one hundred years, that a military training program is academically deficient is not too persuasive. I do not know of any evidence that it is comparatively inferior to the core courses of physical education. In any event, grades toward graduation should be given only in academically approved courses. It is the question of excluding the program that is being dealt with here. Of course it still continues on a number of campuses and that is one reason that the problem may be again presented.

The Cleaver Course

An interesting illustration of a combined curricular-employ-ment problem involved Mr. Eldridge Cleaver and a course desig-nated Social Analysis 139 X, "Dehumanization and Regeneration in the American Social Order," offered fall 1968 at the University of California at Berkeley. The University's academic senate approved the course under a delegation of authority from the Regents "to authorize and supervise all courses and curriculum," the delegation originally to be exercised through committees of the senate. The Regents, however, had specifically retained the authority to make appointments to the faculty.

The course approved by the appropriate faculty senate com-mittee provided that Mr. Cleaver would give ten of the twenty lectures, the balance to be given by at least eleven different faculty members and community leaders, supplemented by section meetings. Five credits toward graduation were allocated to the course. When the Regents became aware of the course, they adopted a resolution stating that "no one may lecture . . . for more than one occasion during a given academic quarter on a campus for University credit, unless he holds an appointment with the appropriate instructional title." Moreover, they resolved, "If Social Analysis 139 X cannot be restructured to satisfy the policy . . . prior to commencement of instruction in the Fall Quarter . . . [it] shall not be offered for credit." These resolutions were adopted well before the opening of the fall quarter.

The course was given, but not brought into conformity with the Regents' resolutions. Noting that the course was under way, the Regents passed an additional resolution that 139 X "not be given credit either directly or indirectly." Subsequently, a long-established independent-study course designated Psychology 198 was offered in a manner to include recognition for credit of the work that was done in 139 X. Students were refused credit in both courses.

The legal point dealt with the question of delegation. The

university's position, upheld by the courts, was that the faculty senate had made an appointment to the faculty when it designated a person to conduct one-half the course, an area "clearly reserved to the Regents." In other words, the delegation to authorize courses did not include the power to appoint faculty. But if such a power had been delegated, it was "neither exclusive nor irrevocable," because the Regents had reserved, as required, their ultimate right to govern.

This concept is extremely important in a situation where full powers of organization and government are vested by constitution or statute in a board of trustees. They can take back or modify what they have given. To delegate is not to surrender authority. As for the Psychology 198 course, it was held to be a "transparent device" to provide indirect credit and therefore also failed.

The expressed theory of the Regents was that they had to act in order to preserve the integrity and quality of the university faculty. This was hardly complimentary to the faculty but it was not intended to be. Unquestionably, it was the record and militancy of Eldridge Cleaver that concerned the Regents, the image of the university that they believed he would convey to the state legislature and the people of the state, and the stream of press comment and angry letters that provoked their actions. If a Ralph Bunche or a Senator Edward Brooke had been invited to give ten or twenty lectures in a political science course, for credit, it is doubtful whether the Regents would have passed the two-lecture no-credit rule.

Mr. Cleaver did not help the situation. At a student rally held before the commencement of the courses, he advised the students that they had no recourse but to take to the streets if the Regents blocked 139 X. He would lecture, he said, "as long as the students and as long as the faculty can stand my profanity." The course enrollment started with one hundred for "credit" and four hundred auditors. Lectures were scheduled once a week.

According to report, obscenities were liberally distributed throughout his first lecture on racism. By the fourth lecture he had fewer students and used the student union for a teach-in in which he criticized those seeking credits as playing establishment games.

The course was part of an experimental series; it was intended in part to give an insight into the racial attitudes of a hot, black soul on ice and the forces that formed them. It was experimental and was the program of an education development board, a new small committee of the academic senate. The right of the Regents to withhold credit under the circumstances was only one aspect of the case. Was the right wisely exercised? The weight of public opinion approved—the Regents had forestalled a foolish faculty error. Many faculty disagreed and believed that the course was imaginative innovation, with a positive educational potential. A third view was that a mistake in judgment had been made, but that it would have been better for the cause of innovation if the course had been allowed for credit and the faculty senate as a whole had been given the time to evaluate it. The assumption was that they would have sternly brought down the curtain on this type of course conducted by a nonqualified leader and prohibited a repetition.

Certainly the resolution of the matter through administration and faculty would have been preferable to confrontation, which zeroed in on the issue of delegation. In any event, it may be that the students had already learned that unrestrained and rambling tirades against society, with an intemperate mixture of truth and untruth, can be boring; such a lesson may be worth more than five credits. Note that the Regents did not prohibit the course, only the credits; free speech was permitted. They did not pass on the course content, but insisted that a course consisting of two or more lectures involved a faculty appointment over which it had reserved jurisdiction.

One cannot say, categorically, that there is never a time when a board of trustees should act in controlling some specific phase of instruction. Certainly if it ascertains that a number of faculty members are substituting discussions of social and political philosophy for their assigned courses in chemistry or engineering, the board can establish or restate a policy that prohibits politicizing in the classroom and require its implementation. But in general the classroom is a sacred place for the exchange of ideas and the board invades this sanctum at its peril.

Trustees should recognize that administration and faculty should handle even the most controversial curriculum matter and afford the opportunity to do so. If action by the board becomes necessary to preserve the educational integrity of the institution, the trustees must take it, knowing, however, that its premise for the need to intervene will be disputed.

Ethnic Studies

The curriculum of black studies has its own peculiar problems. It is probably true that there are black aspects to statistics—statistics relating to black employment, black health, black family life—which apply to no other group. It is clear that the psychological and social problems of the black community and black individuals have a special character, but I dare say that there is more of the general than the particular in all of the so-called black studies. The theories, principles, and techniques of statistics are abstract and general. The human family shares most psychological problems, and political pressures seem to be quite the same whether exerted by white or black groups. It seems to me that the word "black" is used to modify studies principally to indicate identification and emphasis. The black student knows that, to the fullest extent, if black concerns are pertinent to a subject they will be covered. The black seeks to find himself through these studies—to learn where he came from, where he is, where he hopes to go. Understanding his identity, he is better able to cope with his fellow white students in approximately two-thirds of his remaining curriculum.

There are many in academic life and in industry who are against black studies in principle. They feel that knowledge and truth are neither black nor white. A great many courses, they believe, have parts that are of special interest to blacks, but whites should also participate in them if the races are to achieve a better mutual understanding. Statistics, they say, should be given in the economics department; political science, including the special areas of black interest, in the political science department; cultural anthropology should consider differences in culture and general anthropology should tell all students, respectively, where they came from. The history of blacks is part of the history of mankind and should be taught in the history department.

Certainly it must be recognized that, in the past, historians have given insufficient attention to the black experience, black achievements, and black problems. These distortions must be corrected in the history department if they have not already been attended to. But it is wrong to substitute one set of distortions for another—for example, to falsely enlarge some minority contribution far beyond its actual importance. Further, there is danger when studies are isolated that they will omit some of the unpleasant features of their own background. The slave trade is one of the ugliest chapters in the history of mankind, and white men are primarily guilty; but they had help from a great many black tribal leaders. Will this truth be taught in a segregated study? In short, the charge has been made that black studies are divisive, that they fragment knowledge and are designed, however well intended, to give a biased or improperly weighted view of the subject at hand.

The answer given by blacks is that until the university as a whole is equipped to teach a black man and woman from "the inside out" there must be black studies. The issue will be with us for a long time. Probably just as higher education has had to adjust to special admissions for a period of time in order, partially, to right old wrongs, so it will also be necessary to continue black studies, for a time, in the interests of encouraging racial pride and acceptance and providing a classroom forum of greater frankness and candor than is usually achieved when blacks and whites are together and blacks are in the minority. But as black leadership becomes more generally educated, as black professors become more numerous, teaching all academic subjects, we can anticipate that most black studies will ultimately return piece by piece to the general curriculum where they belong.

In any case, black studies must not be collected in a department independent of other departments and schools. Their courses should meet the same requirements for examination, review, and quality as do courses in other departments. If standards are not thus coordinated and upheld, the quality of the black studies program will be inferior and the student will be the one to suffer.

Actually, black students have been rather selective and pragmatic about black studies. In the beginning, the desire for identification was so intense that some black studies departments established a course in Swahili. It did not take long before students recognized that they did not have much use for Swahili. The interest has definitely dropped.

In the same way, students are taking another look at the degree in black studies which many institutions provide. Where will this degree carry them? It will be a credential for ghetto work; it will enable them to serve their people. But there is a great urge among many black students to become part of the mainstream of American life, to participate in its industry, offices, politics, and work. These broader interests are leading and will lead many black students away from a black studies major.

I have been dealing with black studies, but there are other ethnic studies as well. Indeed, in many colleges the black studies department is contained in a school of ethnic studies. Most popular after black studies are the Chicano or La Raza studies. These attempt to do many of the same things for the Chicano community that the blacks seek for their own—namely, a sense of identity, of history, of consciousness of the problems peculiar to that group and ways of solving these problems. Here again there is a strong remedial program, although there is also an effort to conduct part of these studies on a bilingual basis in order to overcome the language deficiency. Yet it should be a cause of grave concern that an ethnic group which has been in the United States for longer than most Americans should not learn English either as a first or second language. Our public schools have a lot of ground to make up.

The American Indian is part of the ethnic studies group, chiefly in the fields of religion, art, philosophy, and history. The subject is sensitive. The white man's record with the Indian is a terrible tale of ruthlessness, greed, and double dealing. Indeed, there is far too much in history of man's inhumanity to man, white to white as well as to the Indian, and other races among themselves and to each other. This is an additional reason to teach history outside of a purely ethnic context—to afford perspective regarding the good and evil characteristic of all human struggle and development and to provide some measure of solace that, hopefully at long last, in the latter part of the twentieth century, mankind is beginning to perceive its essential unity.

The Asian-American studies—Chinese, Japanese, Filipino—have their ethnic academic counterpart. They, too, have courses on practical English skills for Asian-Americans. Most of the studies in the California institutions deal with hyphenated questions—Asian-Americans and the law; Asian-American communities and the urban crisis; mental health problems in the Chinese-American community; the Japanese-American personality; and so on. The principal Asian studies are reserved for art, philosophy, history, and other general departments. Asian-Americans may take one or two courses in the ethnic studies field, but most prefer the general university or college. They are aware of their culture, which has stressed learning values for thousands of years; they do not have the identity crisis that other groups feel, though some are disturbed by their hyphenated status in America.

Black students are usually anxious to exclude white students from their classes. They contend that the presence of a white student changes the discourse; a reference that any black would understand immediately must be explained to the white student, and there is often a lack of candor in view of the presence of an "alien" element. As a legal matter, it is not constitutional for a state university to exclude blacks or whites; and there is some question as to whether a class in certain problems may constitute a sufficiently reasonable classification to exclude any ethnic group. Perhaps it is legally permissible to admit students who have had only a certain kind of prior living experience, say, the black ghetto. Few classes would qualify even under this limited concept. As suggested previously, knowledge should be open to all, and it appears to be erroneous educational policy to impose exclusion on an ethnic basis. Assuredly, it is quite odd to fight so hard for civil rights in many a bloody encounter so that desegregation may be achieved in the public schools, only to advocate academic segregation at the college level.

Usually new programs such as ethnic studies come to trustees for approval if they lead to a degree or require financing. Trustees should assure themselves that certain requirements have been met before an ethnic program is launched or modified or reviewed. They should know the kind of program contemplated, the relationship it will have to other departments and schools, the manner in which the leadership and staff will be selected, and the quality of the program. Student interests and aspirations are important, but they cannot be automatically controlling. The trustees should receive periodic reports which should show that these studies have bona fide academic value and are not curricula designed to encourage divisiveness or to propagandize. They should have clear goals and be related to the principal purposes of the institution.

One of the greatest problems is building up faculty in this field. The number of black Ph.D.s and experienced professors is very small for the area. Indeed, many black Ph.D.s are receiving premium pay, and much unfair raiding of the old established black colleges of the South has taken place. The college or university would do well if it could enlist the interest and understanding of the surrounding ethnic communities when it develops its ethnic programs.

Finally, the trustees should be satisfied that its recruitment procedures for the ethnic programs of the institutions will guard against transferring such programs to the sole control of any one faction of an ethnic group that has particular political and social axes to grind and that has a definitely subordinate interest in education. It will assist the trustees considerably if their board membership includes representatives of minority groups who have an immediate understanding of their minority problems.

Trustee policy toward ethnic studies should recognize, first, that separate ethnic studies programs within the academic framework are presently desirable if they remedy deficiencies in curriculum content, avoid distortions, facilitate identification, and treat ethnic problems, and, second, that ultimately most ethnic studies should be distributed appropriately throughout the general curriculum and be taught by professors on the basis of merit regardless of race, religion, or sex.

Relevance

A good many students consider that their education is not relevant in the context of the problems of society. They are aware of the problems of nuclear weapons, unequal treatment of ethnic groups and women, resentments in the ghetto, hunger among the poor—and then they are made to take a course in Shakespeare or in eighteenth-century literature. They claim it makes no sense. Who cares whether Ophelia was mad or just a little stupid? Why listen to King Lear roaring on the heath? What can men in powdered wigs tell a youngster with an Afro hairdo?

We know that Shakespeare and eighteenth-century literature can tell modern man a great deal. I know an attorney who on several occasions has told parents, on the verge of giving away too much of their property to their children in order to reduce death taxes, about the story of King Lear, the monarch who gave up his properties to his three daughters and lived and died to rue the day. A competent teacher of Shakespeare, knowing the vastness of his understanding of human nature, should have no problem whatever in making Shakespeare as fully relevant to present-day youth as he has been relevant for almost four hundred years. Indeed, he was so relevant in France during the World War II occupation that the Germans prohibited a presentation of *Coriolanus* for fear that it would cause an anti-occupation riot. As for eighteenth-century literature, the sources of all our civil rights, of all our individual freedoms, are embedded in it. Relevance is mainly a matter of good teaching and willing listening. Of course, if all life began in 1952, everything preceding is irrelevant.

Nevertheless, students do have a legitimate complaint about the rigidity of curricula—the course requirements prerequisite to and for their major studies. They see the liberal arts program as designed to produce nineteenth-century ladies and gentlemen.[2] They feel that curriculum changes should be made that will better fit them for life in the age of nuclear threat, poorly distributed housing, environmental struggles, and other pressing social issues.

Higher education is beginning to respond to this demand in providing curricula in environmental studies and the dynamics of social change. Also, many institutions have discovered that field work in social and community agencies motivates students to study. These internships in the community are most valuable because they lead to an understanding of the many facets of a single social problem. Some faculty have been slow to adopt these new procedures.

Trustees have been sympathetic with the idea of changing courses to cover the current scene; they tend to approve the practical

[2] Yet liberal arts can be broadly presented and may be the best preparation for self-development and enjoyable use of leisure time.

and they can see merit in a direct approach to relevance. What trustees are concerned about is that courses dealing with current political, economic, and social issues be fairly taught. They want relevance to be interpreted in terms of the total picture, not part of it. If this is the purpose, they would do well to encourage faculty to bring into the classroom as visiting lecturers the leaders of government and community agencies who are coping with these problems on a day-to-day basis. The students should go into the field, and field superintendents, executives, welfare and human relations workers should come to the students. Knowledgeable government and community leaders may help to show the positive as well as the negative aspects of social issues: what has been and is being done and the planning for the immediate future, what the problems are and what in their opinion is needed. This is not to delegate the teacher's responsibility to the visiting lecturers but to use experience as a test for theory and to seek such truth as may be found in the marketplace. The generation gap may be narrowed if the generations are brought together in the classroom.

Trustees should recognize that the demand for relevance of subject matter to modern life is valid to a considerable extent, and that meeting it requires skilled and imaginative teaching; the elimination of unnecessary requirements; and recognition of the educational and credit value of field and other outside experiences of the student.

Counseling

Unquestionably, there is too little counseling in the high schools. Existing counselors must each deal with five hundred or more students; consequently, their guidance must be of the sketchiest kind. Trustees should alert their coordinating councils, legislators, and state boards of education to this problem and do whatever they can to bring about more adequate counseling services in the high schools.

They can also ask their administration and faculty to improve counseling within their own institutions. Almost every student has a faculty advisor, but he soon discovers that his fellow students frequently know more about courses, programs, and potentials. The faculty member assigned to these duties does not prepare for them as he should: to do so, he should know a good deal about curricula, about professions and vocations in both short and full supply, about sources for student financial aid, and about how to evaluate a student's interests and needs. This is a most valuable service, and the time spent on it should definitely count as a fulfillment of his professional obligations.

One great limitation in this field is the lack of reliable manpower data. There should be a single state agency gathering and distributing information concerning manpower needs over the short and long term, and this material should be available to all counselors and through them to all students. Is there a surplus of engineers, chemists, lawyers, elementary and secondary school teachers? Where does the demand seem to outrun the supply—in health services, in social work, in teaching ethnic studies? The purposes of making reliable information available is not to direct the student to any specific avenue of employment but to give him the basis for making a decision. If the condition of the market in his vocation or profession seems overcrowded, but the chance for instruction is available and he wants to take it, he should be allowed to do so. We have had many instances where apparent oversupply has been converted overnight into undersupply—mathematicians, engineers, and physicists, for instance—and just as quickly the situation has been reversed. Still, a student is entitled to know the probabilities and the prospects.

In the summer of 1972, a survey ("California Supply and Demand for College Educated Manpower in Selected Occupations")¹ was made for a select committee that was reviewing the California Master Plan for Higher Education. According to this survey, fields of engineering, teacher education, and chemistry appeared overcrowded in California. Law was found to offer opportuity but in no way commensurate with the vast number of applications for admission to law schools. The health and welfare services, on the other hand, seemed to afford the great opportunities for employment in the seventies. However, the researchers warned that all data must be pieced together and that what the state requires is a centralized agency to provide continuing manpower data for higher education, industrial, and other public uses.

The conditions in California are probably not unique, and

centralized manpower data on a state-by-state as well as on a federal basis would be most helpful to all students faced with decisions about their futures. As indicated, such data need not be deciding factors. For instance, a student may wish to obtain a law school education for purposes other than to practice law. This is bound to be the result in any event, since the number seeking law degrees is out of proportion to any reasonable estimates of future demands. But no harm can come from more people knowing what the law is and how it is administered and enforced; since every person is presumed to know the law it will be constructive if fact does a little catching up with fiction. And it is true that legal training can be supportive of many kinds of business, government, or professional careers.

The trustees should support the principle of informed academic and career counseling by budgetary allocation, by allowing credit to faculty for counseling services, and by urging the creation of a single state agency to provide manpower data for higher education.

Improvements and Innovations in Instruction

The use of innovative techniques depends somewhat on the basic approach of higher education to mass education. More and more it is recognized that funds for higher education are not unlimited but—in the public sector, at least—must compete with other important public needs in the fields of health, welfare, housing, and transportation. In California over 70 percent of high school graduates go on to some form of higher education, and the proportion is increasing in varying degrees in other states.

Institutions of higher education can take care of additional students by expanding their lecture and laboratory classes and by using fewer professors and more teaching assistants and television. Closed-circuit television can be used to reproduce lectures in other classrooms, and sections led by graduate students can hold discussion sessions. Another approach is to cut down materially on lectures and laboratory classes and substitute increasing home assignments, divide up the students into seminar or tutorial groups, and perhaps reconstitute the curriculum in such a way that a more concentrated educational program is provided in a much shorter time than the generally established program. California State University at Long Beach is contemplating the establishment of a weekend college— providing all of its classes during the weekend in doses sufficiently large to enable students to graduate in four or five years.

More familiar is the trend toward creating "universities without walls." These are extended degree programs conducted through television or correspondence with packaged assignments. The student returns term papers and participates periodically in an on-campus seminar, but he receives most of his education at home. The television instruction may be broadcast over any open channel, but credit is given only to enrollees who perform the necessary assignments and take the required examinations.

The great advantage of the university without walls is that it allows the student to work and still obtain an education. The student is on his own and must be self-disciplined. It is not easy to keep a rendezvous with a particular instructional television program while other interests and demands compete. The shut-in, the older adult with leisure who wishes to achieve a college education, the job-holder who wishes to upgrade himself, the determined young student will succeed in this project. But we can expect that only the most dedicated and highly motivated people will climb to the top of the university without walls. The culturally disadvantaged will not have the environment that will enable them to carry through and up in this kind of independent study. It is extension education at its best; it may help any number of students to improve themselves or complete courses left unfinished, but it will demand great changes in personal habits before it can replace, in any great part, the physical facilities of a going university or college.

Of course, most education is self-education; it cannot be inserted, poured in, vaccinated, or otherwise externally imposed. But it is also substantially the result of exchange and the impacts of personalities on each other. The human dimension provided by teachers and fellow students is extremely important. The university without walls must develop in a way to maintain some of these human relationships. Otherwise it will be an impersonal, cold, intellectual experience. Call-in television or teacher-radio response programs, in which teachers may discuss some student questions for the benefit of all, cannot provide the complete answer. The teacher must not become Big Brother. The university need not put up a wall, but it must have some house where its students occasionally can meet.

There is a further possibility for dealing with mass education which has hardly been touched. This is on-site education at business and industrial establishments. There may be limits to the facilities now available, but the time may well come when a business or industrial establishment will have a number of rooms for its employees engaged in after-work education. A teacher from a university will be brought to the students rather than the other way around. Even if the fields of instruction are limited, the value of such instruction can be considerable. Employee students, who are usually highly motivated and seriously interested in self-improvement, can learn higher skills and be upgraded or make up cultural deficiencies they feel they have.

Most innovations, however, will occur on the college or university campus and many will relate to the period for obtaining a degree. The objective is to permit the student to proceed at his own pace. This procedure recognizes the increasing maturity of students in the 1970s and is designed to eliminate waste, dullness, and repetition in the college curriculum. On the other hand, if there are courses in which the student is experiencing difficulty, the process enables him to proceed at a slower pace according to his own talents and abilities or for personal reasons to drop out and return.

There are a number of techniques that enable a student to complete his education more quickly. He may receive advanced placement in higher education by being given credit for outstanding grades in high school courses of college scope and quality. On the basis of independent study, travel, or other educational experience, he may try passing an examination in a challenged subject without attending a single class and thus, upon passing, receive credit for the challenged course. The theory is that higher education should reward performance, not simply attendance. Credits may be given for certain kinds of work experience such as internship in a public agency or work in a hospital or medical office. The program of general education may be reduced to three years in some if not all of the humanities—if it can be done in Europe, it can be done in the United States.

A combination of procedures can be made available:[3] the large introductory lectures in basic subjects might be given by distinguished scholars over television and the more specialized courses in the customary manner, followed by comprehensive examinations in a large subject area. In the various techniques just mentioned class contact hours are reduced, but the student is given more opportunity to proceed on his own.

Instructional technology now available should be used where it conserves faculty time and adds variety to the learning process. Faculty time should be saved for individual consultations with students about their specific problems. Along with television and radio there are cassettes, playback machines (particularly for language courses), and computer machines for all kinds of data and information. Television, for example, can be far more constructive than any number of lectures in an education class, where it can enable hundreds of students to observe a kindergarten in action, the responses of the children, and the different teaching techniques used. Similarly, television screens can show what is happening in a chemistry lab experiment which could not normally be seen by most students in a lecture hall. In the playback machine the student can hear his own voice speaking a foreign language and compare it with the record of the teacher linguist. The machine does not intimidate the student; it is neutral. But it would be a dreary world if education were dominated by a machine process. The teacher must control the machine.

I suspect there is simply no substitute for a willing student and a stimulating teacher. There is no substitute for motivation in a cultural and intellectual climate or environment. I doubt whether until recently there were many language machines in Hungary, but there are any number of Hungarians who speak six languages. The same is true of the rest of Central Europe, where to survive one must speak (after a fashion) several languages. Machines can help

[3] A number of provocative projects are contained in the proposal of the California State Colleges to the Carnegie Corporation (publication of the Office of the Chancellor, September 1970).

in mass education; they are aids not to be neglected. But the A student will succeed with or without most of them, except where use of a computer can save endless hours of tedious and largely unproductive work.

The trustees can play an important role in the area of innovation. They can inquire of the administration what innovations have been made in the past five years, what are planned, and which require special funding. If the administration and faculty are alert to current developments, such reports should come to the trustees in a routine fashion. But there are times when faculty members drag their feet when new directions should be taken, and the administration is reluctant to force the issue. The trustees, by showing their interest, can awaken the activity and interest of faculty and staff.

Assuming that some important innovations are being implemented, it is particularly important to procure progress reports and periodic evaluations. (Ten percent of the cost of innovative programs is a reasonable sum to devote to evaluation). In two or three years' time it should be possible to know whether a new program is promising or disappointing. Trustee interest will compel attention to detail and to a comparison between practice and theory.

Trustees should keep abreast of innovations in other institutions. If these innovations have no counterpart in the trustees' institutions, they should know the reason. If it is due to lack of funds, then the trustees should ask for a report on the various possibilities for innovation under outside financing. In the competition for foundation assistance, creative programs have the best chance. The Carnegie Commission has published several reports dealing in whole or in part with new techniques in all of the categories discussed and in others.[4]

It will be prudent, of course, to avoid plunging into a new program on a grandiose scale. Innovations that claim to reduce cost but maintain quality may not live up to their expectations. A new program is best tested by a pilot project before large commitments are made that may change the very nature of the institution,

[4] *Less Time, More Options: Education Beyond the High School; Change in Educational Policy: Self-Studies in Selected Colleges and Universities* (by Dwight R. Ladd); *Academic Degree Structures: Innovative Approaches* (Stephen H. Spurr).

perhaps for the worse. Change for the sake of change is often not productive.

One point seems clear. No great industry worthy of its name can operate without a research and development fund to keep it abreast of expanding knowledge and new possibilities of doing old things better or adopting new and constructive programs. The knowledge industry is no exception. Indeed, the amazing fact is that so little has been done in investigating superior techniques of instruction and methods of evaluating teaching performance in order to bring out the full potential of individual students. Certainly 2 percent of an annual budget (some say it should be 5 percent) is not too much to devote to research for the purpose of improving the educational process, and almost every institution should provide such a fund.

In considering reports on programs of innovation the trustees should ascertain the extent to which students accept them— that is, how many students have participated and what their reactions and achievements have been compared with use of more traditional methods. The trustees should also determine whether the innovations have extended the benefits of higher education to previously untapped student and community interests; they should learn how applicable the innovations are to improving educational opportunities for minorities and disadvantaged students. Further, they should, to the extent feasible, find out the comparative costs of innovative methods and past procedures. And most certainly they should be concerned with the quality of education provided through innovations. This will not be easy because differences in educational results cannot be ascertained by mere quantification. But unless the faculty and administration can apply some generally acceptable standards, the governing board will have no idea whether it is moving forward or backward in the implementation of its institutional goals.

The trustees should encourage administration and faculty to provide innovations in admissions, degree requirements, acceleration of the period to obtain a degree, independent study, continuing education, methods of instruction and work study, and use of technological aids that will motivate and challenge students of diverse backgrounds to do quality work in higher education. Trustees can be helpful in reviewing proposals, inquiring about recent innovations in their own and in other institutions, supporting requests for appropriations for research and development and for grants, authorizing pilot projects, requiring and evaluating periodic in-depth progress reports and insisting that the human element control the machine.

Improvements in Teacher Training

Most trustees are sympathetic to any program that promotes good teaching. "Good teaching," in fact, has become almost a slogan. The faculty and administration are directly charged with achieving this important objective, but there are certain positions the board may take to help realize it.

First, the board can act to try to make the salary schedules and fringe benefits of the institution competitive. Trustees of public institutions should try to persuade their legislatures to indicate approved salary levels early enough in the spring session so that their recruitment will be effective for the fall. They should authorize the establishment of a system of salaries and promotions which recognizes teaching merit and does not reduce all salary adjustments to a common level of seniority.

Second, trustees should encourage their own faculty members, if they are engaged in training college and university instructors, to require their doctoral candidates to take courses in teaching methodology. At least they should take a general course dealing with the organization of lectures, the most effective techniques of delivery, the use of imagery and examples, and modes of expression most effective with student audiences. A second course would deal with the most effective forms of presentation adapted to the field in which the candidate plans to teach.

These courses will be more effective if they are combined with supervised field work for teaching fellows and assistants so that they would tie in with classroom experience. This is not a revolutionary concept. All public school teachers go through field training; lawyers take courses in trial practice; doctors have supervised residencies; student ministers are given small congregations. Only college teachers are supposed to be born, not made. The best ones undoubtedly are, but most are made and could gain by such formalized instruction.

The Board can also encourage faculty to make self-evaluations and to determine the criteria for the "good teacher." In this regard, a Yale University faculty ad hoc committee listed four criteria for determing an excellent teacher.[5]

First, he has certain qualities of mind: he is an original thinker, has strong curiosity, is critical and self-critical, is logical and analytic, and has a capacity for synthesis. "To qualify for excellence in teaching," the report said, "a candidate should show evidence in the classroom, in his public work, and in other ways, of possessing at least one of these qualities to a high degree, and one or two others to a moderate degree."

Second, he is skillful in making presentations: he is capable of clear exposition and accurate and well-planned explanations; he is alert and flexible and can think on his feet.

Third, he appeals to students: he can touch them and get his ideas across; he can appeal "to students of all kinds and all degrees of experience"; he may be a scholar who in low key "can kindle genuine curiosity."

Finally, he can work with students: he cares for his students, gets their papers back on time, shows concern for them as persons, gives them the "feeling that they matter," and shows courage and honesty in dealing with them.

Let the faculty of your institution come up with their own criteria for the excellent teacher. It will help in the recruitment and retention of a competent faculty.

Trustees should encourage faculty to use or develop one or two courses on teaching methods for those planning to become teachers in higher education and to develop and apply criteria for teaching excellence in connection with recruitment, promotion, and tenure. Trustees should reward teaching merit in their salary programs.

[5] *Teaching in the Humanities (Some Criteria of Excellence): Humanities Advisory Committee Report, 1966–1967.*

8

ACADEMIC
FREEDOM

The first expectation of faculty is that the trustees will defend the faculty member's right to individuality and freedom. This concept, which the faculty considers the hallmark of the institution, is more usually known as academic freedom. There are any number of definitions of this right, but they all come to the same purpose— namely, that the teacher must have the right to publish his findings or utter his statements without fear of reprisal in any form.

The claim to this right goes back to the ecclesiastical influences on later universities. The teacher wanted to be protected from any accusation of heresy so that the experience of Galileo would not be repeated. If, the teacher believed, one discovered a scientific fact that was at odds with contemporary thought or with accepted tradition, he should be free to express it, and no power of church or state should have the right to inhibit it. The same applied to new philosophical ideas or conceptions of history or politics. It did not matter that the new idea was unpopular or that it contradicted prevailing belief; it need only express the truth as the faculty member

98

saw it. Thus, as far as the teacher was concerned, the classroom became a sanctuary. Whatever was said or discussed in the classroom was privileged. Indeed, British teachers were protected in France even while France and England were at war.

Defending Unpopular Exercises

By and large boards of trustees have come to respect the claim of academic freedom in the classroom and in publication. They may not always like it, but they accept it. Sometimes they have found it difficult to live with, as in the case of Herbert Marcuse, the philosopher who approves of violent revolution, and who for many years taught at the University of California at San Diego.

In recent years the uniqueness of academic freedom has disappeared because of the widened interpretation given the right of freedom of speech under the First Amendment. Courts now hold that it is unlawful to discharge a teacher for exercising his citizen's right of free speech. Thus, some professors have concluded that the principle of academic freedom is not as important as it was previously and that the trustee's interest in it has become irrelevant.

But in practical terms the concept seems to be as important as it ever was. Every attempt to restrict this right will not and cannot go to court. In a public university if a legislative committee inquires into an alleged abuse of academic freedom in the classroom, it may take no direct punitive action against the teacher whose statements or class operation may have offended them. But in indirect and subtle ways they can punish the institution—for example, by reducing the appropriation for the institution or that curriculum area in which the so-called offense occurred. In such a case, trustees may still have the duty to defend an unpopular exercise of academic freedom before the public and the legislature. They seldom do, but if they did they would establish a relationship with faculty that would serve the institution well.

But in other areas involving the defense of academic freedom, the faculty itself has been at fault. From time to time disruptions have occurred in classrooms because radical students disagreed with a professor's political statement as being too conservative or too establishment. On one occasion on a California campus the din was sufficient to prevent the professor from giving his lecture. Ultimately, the administration, by filing complaints and causing arrests to be made, enabled the professor to continue with his class. The faculty senate, however, issued only the mildest protest, and the faculty generally did not raise the banner of academic freedom to defend their colleague's right to speak. In this affair the board of trustees was deeply concerned and so expressed itself. A faculty that desires its trustees to protect utterances considered to be liberal must be equally defensive of utterances considered to be conservative.

Trustees should be willing to defend an exercise of academic freedom that is unpopular with the public. But, correspondingly, the faculty should be willing to defend an exercise of academic freedom that is unpopular with the faculty as a whole.

Pseudo-Claims of Academic Freedom

The issue of academic freedom in the classroom seems comparatively simple. Yet there are situations when classroom teaching may not be protected by academic freedom. During the height of the controversy about the first great invasion of Cambodia from South Vietnam, some professors permitted their students to discuss and protest the actions of the United States in a variety of classes that had no relationship to the contemporary political scene. The teacher himself would participate wholeheartedly in the condemnation and possibly indicate an activist procedure that could make the protest more effective. It did not matter whether the class was biology, economics, or art. The rationale was that the classroom must be made relevant to the issues of the day and that the college or university should be reconstituted—that is, politicized—in order to lead the government in a change of policy.

The news media were particularly critical of this development, and boards of trustees were obliged to repudiate the idea that academic freedom was involved. It was apparent that both students and faculty in many cases were confused by the two concepts of free speech and academic freedom. Utterances in a biology classroom regarding Cambodia do not violate any constitutional principle of freedom of speech, but the question does not concern freedom of speech. Rather, the teacher is simply abandoning his contractual commitment in the classroom: he is conducting a rap session on Cambodia, when he was appointed to teach biology. His right in the classroom to examine any number of theories and facts in biological science does not cover the entirely different subject of the virtue or evil inherent in sending troops over the Vietnamese border. There are professional responsibilities tied to the exercise of academic freedom.

Responsible faculty bodies—including the AAUP—have issued statements condemning politicizing activities in the classroom. However, an issue of this kind is not dead. Given circumstances of some unpopular political decisions of government, the problem could arise again, and trustees should be prepared to repudiate the pseudo-claim of academic freedom involved in changing the nature and purpose of academic courses in the classroom. At the same time, they should not forget their obligation to protect an unpopular use of academic freedom in the classroom.

A qualifying word: the protest against the Cambodian invasion should be considered against a larger background. During a local or national calamity, classes have been frequently dismissed. Students will leave their classes to help fight a forest fire close to their college town, or to put out the flames that threaten town and campus, as happened in Berkeley in the early 1920s. Students stopped attending classes in Florence, Italy, when flood waters from the Arno ripped into museums and archives, and they spent three weeks drying and salvaging the books. Schools and colleges have been dismissed early so that students could harvest and conserve a crop. In all of these situations, an emergency had to be met, and the educational authorities cooperated to the end that the students who performed for the civic welfare would not be penalized for their community service. Obviously, the emergency was more important than the immediate educational process.

Similarly, a national policy may become of such overwhelming importance, and its effects felt so directly, that holding routine classes may become almost impossible. A missile confrontation that could end the world, a declaration of war by or against us would shatter the composure of any classroom. Students would need an emotional outlet, and quite likely would use biology or whatever class they happened to be in as a place for discussing the events,

even though they had little to do with the course subject matter. A
sensible teacher, seeing the perspective and agreeing that fundamental and compelling factors were at work, would permit the
pressures to be released in such discussion; he would yield to the
human demands of the moment. In effect, the class would be dismissed in place.

But this is a far cry from reconstituting the class in biology
in further sessions as a politically activist cell, with the professor as a
participant, in order to change military, political, or economic
policy at some operating level of government. This objective may
still be pursued, through assembly, demonstration, petition, elections, and the political process—by students and by professors—but
not through the means of the biology class or any other class. To
declare a recess at the time of impact is one thing; to redirect education, to substitute political action for the biology course, is quite
another. Board policy should prevent only the latter procedure. Assuming the Cambodian invasion was an event believed by many
students to be of world crisis proportions, it still would have to be
treated within these principles as justifying at most a kind of recess.

*Trustees should repudiate the pseudo-claim of academic free-
dom when a teacher substantially changes a course to a program
outside his field and abandons his contract.*

The Beard

A true case of academic freedom in the classroom occurred
in 1967 when the play *The Beard* by Michael McClure was performed on the campus of California State College at Fullerton. The
professor in charge of the dramatics class had permitted the students
to produce this play. They had asked to do so because of the
"difficult production problems involved."

The Beard was indeed somewhat difficult to produce. While
it had only two characters, Billy the Kid and Jean Harlow, they
were engaged in one long interplay of suggestion, flirtation, and
encounter, which was bound to end up in a sexual act. The language
used by both characters was highly flavored, four-lettered, and
seductive, and the play does indeed end up with a simulated sexual
act. The play had been permitted to run in San Francisco by a trial

court after a preliminary suspension by the San Francisco Police Department. It had been presented at other universities. To produce it without offense was the problem.

At Fullerton the play was conducted as a laboratory experiment, in a class in drama directing, as a challenge to the director's skill and competence. The actor and actress, both graduate students, had been given their parents' permission to play their parts even though the students were adults. The director was also a graduate student. The instructor of the class was a senior professor who had advised the student that he thought the play was a poor one but had permitted him to conduct the project as a class exercise.

The instructor took particular precautions regarding the audience. Only drama students and their friends in the community were to be admitted, and by passes signed by the instructor, who planned to inform the proposed guests of the nature of the play so that they could decide whether they wished to see it. However, one person who procured tickets gave them to newspaper reporters—and that was sufficient to blow up the class project into a statewide news story and a first-rate legislative issue.

On this occasion the chancellor and the president of the state college were united in defending the project. The president, Dr. William B. Langsdorf, criticized the instructor, first, for permitting a student to proceed with a play he felt was a poor one and, second, for failing to limit the audience to persons who were prepared and properly oriented. But he then went on to say (in testimony before the California State Senate Investigating Committee):

> The responsible conduct of higher education is not an easy thing. It requires exploration of ideas of all sorts, many very unpopular and sometimes risky for the faculty who do so. Yet our free society's life and future depend on such continued challenging and testing. This is called academic freedom; it has constitutional protection. To limit the right to explore and challenge would soon erode all our freedoms.
>
> I believe much of the public criticism in this instance is based upon two misunderstandings. The first is the belief that our students are comparable to public school children.

Only forty-one freshmen are under eighteen, and of course, service in the armed forces is possible at seventeen. The average age of our nine thousand students is over twenty-six. The second misconception is that a college or university is today an ivory tower apart from the world, in which young people can be protected from the ills and the evils or dangerous ideas of society at large for four or more years. This is less true than ever before. To create an artificial environment in the college can only lead students to cynicism regarding the hypocrisy of an institution which claims it searches for the truth, and all of it. It may be wiser for society to have its young adults in contact with perhaps objectionable ideas and concepts under professional supervision, where they can learn to reject them if reason does not support them, rather than to learn them in the gutter as forbidden fruit. I believe it was Thomas Jefferson who maintained that our form of free society, to survive, must tolerate error so long as reason is free to combat it.

The Senate investigating committee did mean business and introduced bills to hold the president personally responsible for anything that occurred on a campus; to require two-thirds of the Senate to reconfirm a trustee after he had served half his term; to limit certain artistic or dramatic programs on campus; to require that all events and meetings on campus be open to the public and to press; and to extend the probationary period for faculty. Other efforts were made to cut support funds for drama and art departments in the budget. All of the bills and amendments were defeated, but the budgetary items came through without a vote to spare.

Although requested by resolution of the Senate, the trustees took no action to penalize the faculty involved. The local campus advisory board gave full support to the president.

Subsequently, in a review presented at the annual meeting of the American Association of State Colleges and Universities Dr. Langsdorf pointed out that our colleges are subject to attack by the extreme right off campus and the extreme left on campus. In the case of rightwingers, he said, "if they cannot obtain control of higher education, dictate its content, and severely circumscribe academic freedom, they would like to destroy it by undermining public confidence and reducing financial support." New leftists attempted to use pornography to shock a college, he said, then place it "in the awkward position of defending itself against infringement of academic freedom, whether it has been used responsibly . . . or irresponsibly." If the legislature cracked down as a result, it was of no concern to the new left since it would have succeeded in polarizing society and the academic community.

President Langsdorf conceded that perhaps a mistake in judgment had been made—that it was not essential that this play, among all the others available, had to be approved for the class. But at all times, the project, even if mistaken, was intended for the classroom, he said—and on the basis of academic freedom, the right to perform the play had to be defended. There had been pressure to compel the president to suspend or discharge the professor or his superior in the academic hierarchy. To have permitted punitive action of this kind would have indeed been to invade the free marketplace of the classroom.

Spater Sculptures

Mr. William Spater was a student in the Art Department of California State College at Long Beach. The curriculum required him to complete a creative art project, and his thesis work consisted of a group of nine or ten pieces of sculpture—life-size nude figures made from plaster or wax. The bodies were painted dark gray and appeared covered with dust. Several were depicted touching their sexual organs. In perhaps the most controversial group, a female figure was shown coming out of a television set toward a standing male nude. Most of the other figures related to ordinary objects of the home—a baby carriage, an ironing board, a washing machine. Because the Art Department required that the work of a student given a master's degree be exhibited, arrangements were made to present it in the college art gallery. (Although exhibiting was customary, there were ten occasions when exhibits were not held.)

The sculpture at issue was completed near the end of the fall semester of the 1967–68 academic year. At the beginning of January, Dr. Robert E. Tyndall, dean of the School of Fine Arts at the college, met with Spater and members of his graduate committee to discuss whether the sculptures should be exhibited at the college. The committee reported that Spater had received proper credit for the project and that this grade would enable him to receive his master's degree, but the committee did not recommend for or against a showing. Spater did not object to this report.

A special meeting of the school council then was convened to consider the matter. Immediately after the meeting, Spater told Dean Tyndall that he was anxious to get a "yes or no answer" on whether the exhibition would be held, but that "he did not really care one way or the other what the answer was." On February 1, the chairman of the Art Department informed Spater that the project would not be exhibited on the campus and that the sculptures would be released to him so that he could seek an exhibition elsewhere. Spater received his master's degree and ceased to be a student in February 1968.

In the meantime there was student agitation, particularly from an SDS group, to restore the exhibit. The effort was not successful. On April 1, Spater and a group of students determined that there would be some kind of exhibit. They entered the building where the sculptures were stored, removed them to the lawn area near the Fine Arts building, and set them up in an unauthorized exhibit. Handbills composed by Spater were distributed, stating in part that he treated the showing on the lawn as satisfying the requirements for his master's degree. Some two thousand persons attended, the press and television were notified, and thus the exhibit had a considerable audience. The students shouted, jeered, and booed members of the college administration, disrupting instruction in adjoining classrooms. The college administration terminated the exhibit after two to three hours and the sculptures were returned to storage.

But Spater was not satisfied with a somewhat festive April 1. The next day he appealed the denial "of my master's exhibit." On April 3, he was notified to remove his sculptures from the campus; he sought and was granted an extension of time on April 15 to April 18, but on April 19 he notified the college that he had "deeded full ownership and responsibility" for the sculptures to a number of named members of the faculty and staff of the college.

These sculptures were then distributed in a number of faculty offices, and student consultations with their faculty advisors visibly increased.

From then on, meetings of faculty councils and senates, state trustees, and legislative committees blossomed out all over the state. A faculty meeting on April 24 and 25 (interrupted by 150 students) agreed with Dean Tyndall's decision "unless officially challenged by the Art Department." The faculty of the Art Department met on April 26, and adopted a resolution requesting that the exhibit be held. On May 2, Dean Tyndall decided to permit the Spater exhibit, limiting persons entitled to view it to students and adults. On May 7, President Carl McIntosh publicly announced that the showing would be held and stated that eligible visitors would be clearly advised that the figures were controversial and that they should not enter if they felt that they would be offended.

On May 14, Chancellor Glenn Dumke and the chairman and the vice-chairman of the State College Board of Trustees appeared before the California State Senate Rules Committee at its request. Senator Hugh Burns, the committee chairman, asked them to "stop the exhibit." The statewide Academic Senate then considered the matter at Chancellor Dumke's request, and the chancellor, together with four trustees, including myself, addressed the Senate. It was our position that the art exhibit was no longer that but had become politicized far beyond its meaning and importance, and that to hold the exhibit currently would be injurious to the college and the state college system as a whole. The Chancellor contended that the reversal by the college administration was the result of confrontation and not deliberation.

The statewide Academic Senate refused to intervene. It said that because the Art Department had pronounced its official judgment, the professional issue had been resolved, and it was all a simple matter of academic freedom. One of the senators quoted John Milton's *Areopagitica* on freedom of thought and expression, and that settled the matter.

By this time the affair had been played up all over the state, and the trustees were deeply concerned that the gray figures of Mr. Spater would deplete the budget figures granted by the legislature to the point of serious injury. The legislators had received pictures of the various sculptures and had distributed them to their colleagues. On May 28 and 29, a violent demonstration of about 250 persons occurred at the administration building of the college. The slogan advanced was "Spater must show, Dumke must go." The demonstration was declared an unlawful assembly, and resulted in the arrest of forty-two students and a faculty member; most were found guilty of unlawful assembly and failure to disperse. The leadership for all demonstrations was pretty much the same.

About a year after the whole question was raised, Spater, several professors, and a student filed a petition for a writ of mandate to compel Chancellor Dumke to set aside his ruling barring exhibition of the project. The trial court, having received evidence and hearing arguments, denied the petition. The trial court was upheld on appeal (*Kenneth Appelgate et al., Plaintiff and Appellants* v. *Glenn S. Dumke, as Chancellor,* etc., 25 CA 3rd 304—much of the factual statement regarding the Spater incident is taken from the opinion in this case).

The appellate court did not consider the issue of academic freedom.

> We reach no issue of academic freedom or the right of the statewide administration of the college system to interfere with local decisions on strictly academic matters. Appellant Spater, by the unauthorized exhibit of April 1, and his properly inferred participation in subsequent acts of confrontation, had politicized the matter of the exhibit before respondent exercised his discretion not to permit it. With Spater's concurrence the question of his project had been removed from the Halls of Ivy to the streets. The problem was no longer one of academic value of the project to Spater and to those who might view it, but rather concerned the future of California State College at Long Beach and the entire state college system. In that state of affairs Chancellor Dumke was not only authorized to exercise his power and discretion as the head of the state college system, but would have been derelict in his duty had he not done so.

The Educational Policy Committee of the Board of Trustees had two rather lengthy discussions about the matter, but it came to the conclusion that definitive action rested with the faculty and administration. The opinions expressed by the committee and other board members informally showed that a heavy majority favored deferring the exhibit at least until the following semester. In the words of Mr. Theodore Meriam, then chairman of the Board of Trustees: "To permit the exhibit of the Spater sculptures . . . can produce far more serious conflicts . . . than have accrued to date in the series of events surrounding these sculptures."

My own statement to the State Academic Senate was as follows:

> The reason for Dean Tyndall's original position, I think, and the views of those [trustees] who are here, is that the project should not be displayed because of the injury that will be sustained by the Art Department, California State College at Long Beach, and the state colleges generally. . . . What I genuinely fear is a spate of restrictive and inhibitive legislation, on the basis that we're unable to govern ourselves. If all this were in a great cause, I would defend it to the point of resignation, but it isn't. It is simply to impose an exhibit of unproved pieces of art, owned by forty-three or more private persons, admittedly offensive to many, in a hotly charged atmosphere which has completely eliminated the possibility of an art exhibit.

More than twenty punitive bills were introduced and barely beaten; unquestionably, several would have passed if the exhibit had not been "deferred." Certain of the bills are referred to in the discussion of *The Beard*. Notwithstanding the cancellation, reviews appeared in several newspapers. The *Long Beach Independent-Press Telegram* thought the exhibit was a rather poor showing of protest art. Mr. William Wilson, writing in the *Los Angeles Times* (June 9, 1968), stated:

> The issue [is] of explicit sexuality; if precedent is a guide this work is not more explicit than objects commonly shown in public galleries and museums to adult audiences. At times Spater seems to say that some neurotic people sub-

limate loneliness and frustrated sexual desire into household fetishes. At another moment he illustrates the well-documented psychiatric notion that certain persons sublimate ungratified sexual desires into patriotism or extreme religious fanaticism. Occasionally one senses an impulse to the lyric celebration of love. To me it is sad there is so little of the latter. . . .

Spater's work ought to have drawn the same crowd of fifty tolerant friends, relatives, and fellow students as any other such mounting. Since fuss has made it an issue, I think it ought to be shown to prove the state college system is not ruled by the mentality of little old ladies in tennis shoes or made to blush by a student's sophomoric fascination with sex. The show's opening ought to exclude the following type: small children, those ashamed of their body and its functions, those desiring a beautiful and affirmative statement about love, and anybody who thinks there is anything sexy going on in that gallery.

The state administration's main difficulty was that a number of powerful legislators and many other people had indicated that they thought something sexy was going on in that gallery. In weighing the importance of insisting upon the exhibit against forthcoming appropriations for the support of the state college system, the chancellor and the trustees felt that the pragmatic choice left them very little option. The academic freedom issue had been blurred by activism. The legislature might conclude that the next event would be a striptease in the cafeteria.

Of course, if the Art Department of the college had declared its judgment immediately, and the limited gallery showing had been provided within the "halls of ivy," then the issue of academic freedom would have been presented along the lines of *The Beard*. Whether a relatively small, tolerant group would have attended (as indicated by the *Times*) and the exhibit concluded without incident is a question; certain public and political sensitivities had been aroused by *The Beard*. But the showing would have taken place prior to any unlawful protest, and the campus and central administrations would have been hard put to deny that academic freedom was again involved. Consistency of action would have required that the banner of academic freedom, somewhat tattered, again be waved at a legislative hearing, but this time I am afraid that legislative punishment would have resulted, in fact, in the form of a budgetary cut or the enactment of one or more of the restrictive bills mentioned above. Whether the exhibit of the Spater figures, in principle, would have been worth the price is a matter upon which, fortunately, we do not have to conjecture.

It is possible that a tax-supported institution has to exercise more careful judgment than do private institutions in sponsoring or supporting activities in the performing or visual arts if such displays are likely to antagonize a great many taxpayers and their representatives.

A wise faculty member will not put an institution in the position of testing the limits of public acceptance in the theatrical and art fields if he is not fully convinced of the worth of the experiment. The development of procedures for advance consideration of such projects by responsible faculty and administrative leadership should reduce incidents of extremism to a minimum. Trustees should take care to avoid becoming victims of the techniques of the extreme right or left. When errors in judgment may have been honestly made, however, trustees should defend them as the price of freedom and innovation. In any clear case the trustees must support academic freedom, whatever the legislative consequences.

This is not to say that the public should be denied knowledge of any scandalous conduct in a classroom. The classroom is the place for an exchange of ideas but not for immoral or illegal conduct. I mention the point not because the question of such conduct has been presented in any material way but to make clear that a classroom is not absolutely inviolate from public scrutiny.

College-sponsored or permitted student-art exhibits or performances may offend the public to the point of endangering the support of the institution. The policy of trustees should be to require procedures of consideration and judgment on campus, which should minimize the possibility of unnecessary crises. If an incident does occur, the trustees should try to keep it in context and perspective and defend the cause of academic freedom if it is substantially in-

volved. They should disapprove of bad taste. (Of course, hard-core pornography has no place on the campus.)

Campus Disruption

Some of the most difficult questions of academic freedom occur outside the classroom. What happens if a professor, at a rally, condemns university administrators for failing to insist on relevance in classroom teaching or not admitting enough minority students? What if he leads a protest and presents a petition to the president? What if he tells the students that the time has come to act in accordance with principle and that it may be necessary to demonstrate before the administration building in order to show the force and righteousness of their joint cooperation?

Academic freedom does not seem to be directly involved in any of these instances. As a citizen the professor has the same right as others in expressing himself. He can participate in an assembly and he has the right to join in a petition—these are the citizen's rights of free speech. But if he incites to violence and the students invade and damage the administration building, wholly or partly because of his stimulus and direction, he is no longer protected by the principle of free speech; he has violated the law against incitement to riot. Thus, he is subject to punishment under the criminal laws and also to discipline as a faculty member, in accordance with due process both in the judicial and the faculty-administrative proceedings.

Free speech does not include any right to incite to riot on campus or elsewhere.

The Bruce Franklin Case

Because the 1972 disciplinary case of Dr. H. Bruce Franklin of Stanford University received national attention and focused on several matters of academic freedom previously discussed, I would like to consider it here. Perhaps nowhere in recent academic history have the lines of what is permitted and prohibited been so well drawn.

Dr. Franklin, an associate professor of English at Stanford, is a specialist in the literature of Herman Melville, and his competence as a teacher was nowhere questioned. Nevertheless, the Advisory Board, selected by the whole Stanford faculty, after a hearing recommended his discharge; the university president decided to accept the recommendation and the board of trustees concurred in it.

I have heard professors say about the incident, "It just goes to show you—when the establishment wants to get you, it can." Or, "There's no real freedom of speech; when they get scared, they just close down on a man."

In my opinion, the decision of the Stanford Advisory Board should be read by all faculty everywhere. This is one case that no one should comment or expound upon if what he knows comes only from gossip or newspapers; he should research it himself, if he can.

There were four principal charges to the Advisory Board against Dr. Franklin:

First, when U.S. ambassador to South Vietnam Henry Cabot Lodge spoke at Stanford at a public meeting, Professor Franklin was in the audience and participated in loud shouting, chanting, and clapping, which prevented the ambassador from speaking and which forced the cancellation of the program.

Second, on February 10, 1971, at a noon rally on the campus (with over five hundred persons attending), Professor Franklin, it was specifically alleged, "intentionally urged and incited students and others present . . . to disrupt university functions and business and specifically to shut down a university computer facility known as the Computation Center. Shortly thereafter a large number of students and others left the rally . . . and did, in fact, occupy the Computation Center, prevent its operation, and obstruct movement in and outside of the building for several hours, terminating this unlawful activity only when ordered to leave the building by police."

Third, on the same day, in connection with the activity at the Computation Center, "students and other persons were arrested for failure to disperse after orders had been given to clear an area around the Computation Center. Professor Franklin significantly interfered with orderly dispersal by intentionally urging and inciting students and other persons present at the Computation Center to disregard or disobey such orders to disperse."

Finally, the same evening on campus a rally of two hundred

people was held to discuss, among other matters, ways of protesting developments in the Indochina war. "During the course of the rally Professor Franklin intentionally urged and incited students and other persons present to engage in conduct calculated to disrupt activities of the university and of members of the university community and which threatened injury to individuals and property. Shortly thereafter students and other persons were assaulted by persons present at the rally, and later that evening other acts of violence occurred."

In accordance with Stanford's procedures, the charges were heard by an Advisory Board of seven members elected by the faculty. This board acted on the charges as follows: it unanimously refused to sustain on the Lodge incident; it unanimously sustained the noon rally charge; it sustained by five to two the charge of interference with orderly dispersal; and it sustained by five to two the last charge of incitement to disruptive conduct. These violations, the board found, constituted "substantial and manifest neglect of duty or conduct substantially impairing the individual's performance of his appropriate function within the university community" in accordance with Stanford's policy on tenure. The vote for discharge was five to two; the two minority members recommended one quarter's suspension without pay, and one minority member recommended an additional quarter's suspension with pay.

There were thirty-three days of hearings, and the Advisory Board met for a total of 160 hours and heard testimony from 111 witnesses. The transcript contains about a million words and the decision covers 148 pages. President Richard W. Lyman accepted recommendations of the Advisory Board, including the discharge of Professor Franklin. In approving the recommendations, the President said:

> I wish to call special attention to an issue addressed by both the majority and the minority of the board, namely, the effect of this decision on free speech and academic freedom at Stanford and at other institutions of higher education. It is significant that the issue was a salient one for all members of the board . . . Yet I am convinced that no fair and careful reading of the record of this case will provide comfort for any who may be tempted to use it as precedent

for an attack on the freedoms essential to an academic institution. Chief among these is, of course, the freedom to hold and advocate whatever views one's conscience and knowledge may lead one to have, no matter how unpopular or disturbing to orthodoxy or downright outrageous those views may appear to others, and no matter how large may be the majority that dislikes them. Professor Franklin, in common with all other members of the Stanford faculty, has long enjoyed that freedom. The decision of the Advisory Board rests on the conclusion that on specific occasions in particular circumstances his speech exceeded permissible bounds by "urging and inciting to the use of illegal coercion and violence, methods intolerable in a university devoted to the free exchange and exploration of ideas." My agreement with that conclusion is buttressed by the knowledge that the minority dissent is based on disagreement over the interpretation of fact and motive and over the appropriateness of penalty, *not* on a finding that the University's intention or action in bringing the case was directed against the right of a faculty member to believe and to espouse unpopular views.

The Stanford Board of Trustees, after reviewing a further statement by Professor Franklin, considered the matter and concurred in the president's acceptance of the Advisory Board's decision.

Both the decision and the defense relied heavily on the context as well as the words of the professor's speeches. The Advisory Board found that the circumstances surrounding the speeches "were characterized by overt turbulence and escalating protest activities" concerning the Indochina war. These activities involved attempted arson, rock throwing, Molotov cocktails, the breaking of about one hundred windows, holding a trustee committee under siege for forty-five minutes, and much militant discussion of attacking the Computation Center "both for its alleged war complicity and for its vulnerability." Professor Franklin, as the last speaker of the noon rally, concluded ("with delivery shifted to a high intensity"), "See now, what we're asking is for people to make that little tiny gesture to show that we are willing to inconvenience ourselves a little bit and to begin to shut down the most obvious machinery of war, such as—and I think it is a good target—that Computation Center." The Board found that he had incited unlawful acts. The board said: "Professor Franklin must have reasonably expected that his advocacy of 'shut down' would be interpreted by a least a substantial portion of the audience as calling for forceful disruption of the operation of the Center." (Indeed, after his speech the crowd voted to go to the Computation Center, and two hundred did so. And they closed down the computer, doing about $800 of physical damage, not counting any cost of shutdown.) The board further determined that in his later evening speech Professor Franklin "provided justification for coercive and violent behavior toward the targets of his animosity —the police and the University" and that he intentionally urged and incited his audience to engage in conduct that would disrupt activities of the university and threaten injury to persons or property.

Dr. Franklin contended that he had been misquoted or quoted out of context on all counts, that he had simply advocated a mobile strike or voluntary boycott as a political protest and pursuant to his constitutional rights, that neither his speeches in their entirety nor selected parts could be construed as inciting to violence, and that the University would have to prove that he was communicating with the audience in "a secret language" (inciting to unlawful acts) in order to prove its case. As for the police incident, he claimed that the evidence showed that he had nonviolently attempted to persuade them to retract an unlawful or unwise order to disperse.

Professor Franklin's court action (brought by the American Civil Liberties Union) to obtain reinstatement and damages is pending. His contention is that at all times he was simply exercising his constitutional right of free speech. The trial court thus far has denied the University a summary (immediate) judgment on the record, the issue of a possible trial de novo (that is, without reference to the record) remains. If such a trial is granted, then the University and Dr. Franklin would again present their witnesses and evidence to the court without regard to any prior proceeding, and the hearing before the faculty Advisory Board would be deemed a nullity.

The university contends that at most the court must confine

itself to the record for two purposes: (1) to determine whether Dr. Franklin had a fair hearing (due process) and (2) to determine whether there was substantial evidence to support the conclusion that his speech constituted incitement to violence.

Of course, if the principle adopted is that a faculty member in Dr. Franklin's position is entitled to a judicial trial, irrespective of whether the university hearing was fair or unfair, then the whole academic tradition of a trial by peers goes by the board. The courts, not the faculties, would become the disciplinary bodies for faculty, at least in any case involving a constitutional question, and faculty hearings in such matters would probably be abandoned as useless.

If the judiciary in the Franklin case limits its review to the record and confirms, revises, or otherwise disposes of the case accordingly, then there are several elements in this case and others like it which will remain notable:

First, the critical hearing in this matter (if the record proves controlling) was conducted by faculty representatives, and the resolution of the issues was made by faculty. The decision would not be nearly as significant if the same decision had resulted from a hearing by the administration.

Second, such a hearing committee must be prepared to exercise considerable patience and courage; its members will be beset by all the pressures generated when conduct claimed to be protected by academic freedom or free speech is involved.

Third, a hearing committee must be meticulous about its procedure; in the Franklin case, the hearings were public; the professor had the right to counsel and to examine and cross-examine witnesses.

Fourth, charges in a disciplinary proceeding must be specific and proved. The questions in the Franklin case concerned particular speeches and acts and whether these constituted incitement to engage in disruption of the university process and other unlawful conduct. Any discipline would have to be for the conduct of incitement, not for promoting ideas, popular or unpopular.

Perhaps, as will be set forth in the discussion on tenure, outside hearing officers (instead of a faculty committee) should be used to make findings of fact when these are in dispute in disciplinary cases. The Stanford Senate itself, after a two-year study of guidelines[1] to disciplinary action and procedure, has come to this conclusion. The matter is under consideration by the president and Board of Trustees. In the interest of conserving the time and energy of a university faculty, such a change of procedure may be advisable. But unquestionably the strength of the academic community is better tested if it can handle a difficult issue, such as the Franklin case, on its own.

Fifth, Stanford is a private university (though with several public aspects), and it may be that it could have claimed the right to impose stricter standards regarding faculty rights in speech and conduct than are permissible for public institutions. However, in the Franklin case the faculty board adopted essentially the same standards of permissible speech and conduct as would be applicable to a public institution. This is sound and advisable precedent for any private institution.

Sixth, it is interesting to conjecture what would have happened if the faculty Advisory Board had exonerated Professor Franklin. The president might technically have had the authority to decide against the professor and to discipline him on the ground that the Advisory Board had unreasonably interpreted and applied the standards of conduct required by the university in the light of the record of the case. But the president's position under such circum-

---

[1] According to the recommended guidelines, a professor would be subject to disciplinary sanctions for doing the following: (a) Engaging in professional misconduct in the performance of his academic activities or his duties in connection with the university; (b) neglecting the academic duties that he has undertaken to perform within the university; (c) preventing or obstructing the effective carrying out of a university function or approved activity; (d) obstructing the legitimate movements of any person about the campus or in any university building or facility; (e) inflicting physical harm or other serious harm on any member of the university or anyone on the campus; (f) causing damage or destruction to, or misappropriating, property owned by the university or any of its members or used in connection with any university function or approved activity; (g) violating any university regulation that has been duly promulgated and approved by the senate of the academic council, president, and the board of trustees; (h) refusing to appear and testify when summoned in connection with, or giving false testimony in, any proceeding governed by this statement; (i) attempting the conduct described in (a) through (h) of this section; or aiding and abetting such conduct; or inciting anyone to engage in such conduct; or threatening to engage in such conduct for the purpose of intimidation or extortion.

stances would almost be untenable after such a lengthy and serious hearing. The faculty would not have supported such a reversal unless he returned the case to the same board with persuasive argument and they modified their prior opinion and concurred with him.[2]

Seventh, the position of the board of trustees in this kind of case is simply to be a final but limited court of appeal for the appellant professor. Conceivably the rules of a university could permit the board to review the evidence, hear new evidence, and effect a discharge, notwithstanding the determination of a faculty committee and the president to the contrary. Such an action would place an institution in considerable peril. The faculty and students would probably be outraged. It could happen that faculty and president would have been so irresponsible on the record that the action of the board would be justified and upheld by the courts since the board usually has the final legal authority in governance. But a board that has lost its faith both in its faculty and in its chief administrator is due for rough sailing.

The board of trustees should restrict itself to a review of the record for two purposes: to be satisfied that the procedures followed were in accord with the institution's requirements of academic due process, and to determine whether the penalty should be confirmed, reduced, or rescinded in the light of the facts found by the faculty committee. The board should not place itself in the position of a trial agency, or it may find itself so occupied that it will have to abandon its main functions of governance.

Eighth, as the Stanford Advisory Board perceived it, the great background issue in the Franklin case was the survival of the university. Can a university act to protect its own freedoms? Must it succumb to those whose views, however passionately and zealously held, can be satisfied only if its processes are destroyed? It is the unique position of the extreme left and the extreme right that only they know the truth, only they should be heard, only their solutions must be employed, and that those who disagree with them must be silenced—through threats, disruption, and violence. Such opposition

[2] An exception might occur if the board demonstrated a clear violation of law. Then the president's reversal might stand without faculty concurrence.

is not dissent; it seeks not merely to chill but to kill the intellectual freedom for which the university exists. (Dr. Franklin vigorously denies that Stanford was in any such peril by reason of his speeches; he claims that the university itself was engaged in oppression, in suppressing speech, and in attempting to kill or chill true intellectual freedom.)

Ninth, although the Franklin case deals with incitement versus dissent, a board of trustees is interested in a further aspect of this kind of case—namely, whether a professor must be guilty of incitement in almost a criminal context in order to be subject to discipline. If a professor expressly approves of disruption and violence on campus, without engaging in it, and under conditions in which no danger is present, may he nevertheless have crossed into the area of unprofessional conduct? Suppose he tells students, "If you really believe in a campus cause, you should go all the way, block anybody from attending classes and tear the place down." It would indeed be a thin line—he might advocate violence in general as an instrument for change, but not on the campus.

Yet it is not unreasonable to construe unprofessional conduct as covering the advocacy of injury to the property of the institution or of the physical disruption of the educational process within it, even though such speech may be in general terms and not designed for immediate incitement. A teacher who supports the goal of a rational academic community should support such a principle. The history of campus disruption shows that it does not come out of the blue. It comes in a climate of violence (as opposed to reason). The rule would have to be a professional one. It may present constitutional problems and be open to abuse by tale bearers. Under any circumstances a professor must always be free to criticize in the strongest terms the administration and educational process in his institution.

The academic community should familiarize itself with the Franklin case because it seeks to draw the line between incitement and free speech and because it is illustrative of the problems involved in any large disciplinary action. The community might also consider the adoption and testing of a self-disciplinary policy which would make a faculty member's advocacy of violence on campus a breach of professional conduct (irrespective of whether incitement is involved).

9

TENURE

The concept of tenure has been widely misunderstood in recent years. It has been criticized by younger faculty, legislative committees, and newspaper editorials. National associations of faculty and university groups such as the American Association of State Colleges and Universities have published their analyses and comments about the system. The most recent study is that of the National Commission on Academic Tenure, a committee sponsored by the American Association of University Professors and the Association of American Colleges and Universities, which was financed by the Ford Foundation. The findings of this special commission, on which I was privileged to serve, were published in 1970. Much but not all of what follows is derived from that study.[1]

Because trustees ultimately must establish or confirm the rules of tenure governing the appointment and continued employment of academic personnel, it is most important that they be

---

[1] *Faculty Tenure: A Report and Recommendations by the Commission on Academic Tenure in Higher Education.* San Francisco: Jossey-Bass, 1973.

thoroughly familiar with the values and problems of the tenure program.

Bases of Tenure

In one sense, tenure is a very old idea. The masters of the early British universities had a claim on their offices which could not be set aside or destroyed by the university authorities, despite any "heretical ideas" the masters might have. However, the American application of this principle to faculties is comparatively recent. During the nineteenth century a professor served pretty much at the pleasure of the president and trustees of the institution. In 1900, economics professor Edward A. Ross was discharged from Stanford University because his views offended Mrs. Stanford. President David Starr Jordan tried to cover the motive, but the true situation was quite well understood throughout the campus community. Indeed, the issue had national repercussions, and during the next few years the principle was developed that a senior faculty member could not be summarily removed without having a fair hearing that showed the institution had adequate cause. Thus, the foundation of tenure is freedom of expression—the right to speak and publish in the search for truth without fear of reprisal.

A second aspect of tenure has become just as important—namely, economic security. After a professional has proved his competence to his institution, he is protected in his work in the manner akin to civil service; he cannot be deprived of his economic security without cause. The exceptions are if bona fide institutional changes require the abolition of his position; for example, if the financial conditions in the institution no longer support his department or chair, he may be terminated and no violation of tenure will occur. Or, in a public institution, if the legislature fails to provide funds for a school of engineering, say, that curriculum will be dropped and the professors dismissed. Or, if budgetary cutbacks either in a public or private institution will result in only 80 percent financial support of the academic program, it is obvious that some procedure of priorities will have to be determined and a number of competent teachers not provided for in the revised budget will have to be let go.

Positions may also be eliminated because of a marked falling off of student interest in certain curricula. Student demand for mining at the University of California, Berkeley, so dwindled that the Regents found it necessary over a period of time in the 1950s to eliminate a school that had had a notable history and had made a great contribution to the extractive industry throughout the world. Occasionally, in the multiversities, too many similar operations are established on branch campuses and when the student interest or the manpower requirement is not sufficient to justify the continuance of the operation on a particular campus, it is abolished. Language departments in many institutions have recently been curtailed or liquidated because academic requirements and student interests have changed. All of these curriculum modifications have produced academic casualties.

Although the hold on the position is only as long as the position exists, the vast majority of academic personnel in the United States are covered and protected by some kind of tenure system. Many institutions define the terms of tenure—how it is acquired, what guarantee it offers, how it may be lost—in a contract or appointment form or in a faculty handbook. In many public institutions the conditions of tenure are set forth in statute. In other institutions tenure is more a matter of tradition: after it is awarded, it is "understood" that certain conditions of employment apply, although these conditions are nowhere specified. It may be that after a period of service has been completed, it is accepted that tenure has become automatic, or a letter of appointment will grant tenure but not describe it. Writers attacking the tenure system sometimes indicate that it is ephemeral because of the fine print or the lack of any print at all. But actually, whether the conditions of tenure are described in detail or recognized in practice and custom, the professional faculty organizations are alert to protect it. Any institution that pretends to have it and tries to renege will find that further recruitment of faculty is most difficult and even that its accreditation may be withdrawn.

The principal criticisms of tenure have not related to legal deficiencies or the enforceability of contracts. Rather, they have concentrated on the alleged unfairness of the system to the institution and its students. Younger faculty claim that tenure is simply a device of older faculty to keep them in line during a long probationary period and to deny rather than to give them security. If there are limited tenure spaces available and these are occupied by men in their forties or early fifties, the younger aspirants are discouraged from climbing ladders when colleagues at the top must keep their feet firmly planted on the upper rungs. This situation is indeed serious in some institutions that expanded greatly during the growth period of the sixties and granted tenure rather promiscuously. Now there is a considerable reduction in the growth rate, and the faculty tenure roster is impacted at the upper levels. Women and minorities coming into academic life therefore contend that the system is operating unfairly against them.

Another criticism is that tenure tends to protect mediocrity. The nice fellow who gets along with his senior colleagues will ultimately be admitted to the club, but the questioner and the dissident and the young man with innovative ideas will be too disturbing an influence and in one way or other he will be discouraged from attempting to join or be refused membership. Moreover, it is argued, a department that is oriented in a particular way toward its subject matter—in the education field, in sociology, in philosophy—will seek to perpetuate itself by drawing to it the younger aspirants of similar views. The effect is to make tenure a static influence in the academy.

Perhaps the most frequent criticism is that tenure encourages laziness. Once the professional acquires it, his motivation for hard and original work declines. He repeats the old jokes and the old lectures. He misses many of his classes. He assigns term papers, but he does not read them or mark them with care. The students are being cheated. Nothing is done about it because his peers are reluctant to take disciplinary action for incompetence or neglect of duty.

Finally, there is the criticism that academic freedom no longer needs tenure to protect it. In the past decade, important decisions protecting the freedom to teach and to learn have come from the courts under the First Amendment, not from the faculties and administrations of higher education. Consequently, the elaborate machinery of tenure has become unnecessary or obsolete. The Constitution will protect the professional better than his constituted authorities.[2]

There is an element of truth in all these criticisms. Young, creative faculty will be discouraged in an institution where it is probable that all tenure positions will be filled for many years. When tenure is improperly administered, its beneficiaries may make their positions sinecures. The courts have done much to preserve academic freedom in a number of critical cases. But the National Academic Tenure Commission found, after examining the deficiencies and after considering alternative systems, that the tenure system was preferable to any other, and its shortcomings could be guarded against and in many instances removed if tenure were properly administered. The idea of substituting the courts for further institutional protection of academic freedom seems quite mistaken; litigation is expensive and the burden is on the individual claimant. By and large it is better to be judged by one's peers and within the institutional process.

What are the alternatives? An institution may simply have no tenure. Everyone serves at pleasure, no one is bound, the competition of the marketplace will prevail. The faculty will remain only so long as the students work with them and want them. A few experimental institutions, including Hampshire College in Massachusetts, have begun operations on this principle. However, experience indicates that as idealistic faculty become older they prefer more conventional patterns and more assurance of job protection.

An institution can have quick seniority—say, after a professor has put in a year's service. Collective bargaining contracts in industry provide this kind of protection after thirty to ninety days. But there is substantial difference between a production assembly line

[2] Some opponents of the tenure system are certain that it is being destroyed by historical forces: they believe that academia is losing its prestige and magic spell and both employee organizations and young university personnel are rebelling against what they call privilege and sinecures for the older faculty members; that the unions and the law courts will finish the job and substitute seniority for tenure. What isn't clear is whether these opponents seek a result which, in effect, would establish the same job security after a year or less that tenure confers after five or seven years. (See Robert Nisbet, "The Future of Tenure," *Change,* April 1973.)

and the profession of teaching in higher education. If it would be a mistake to provide a lifetime position after five or seven years, how much greater is the risk after one year? Any significant evaluation of performance is impossible in one year. To the extent research publication is important, there is simply no time in one year; to the extent that teaching effectiveness is to be measured, there is simply insufficient experience in such a short time. The reason for a substantial probationary period in academic life is the uniqueness of the academic enterprise. It takes time to evaluate an individual whose work for the most part must be performed without any direct supervision.

Another proposal seeks a middle ground, the so-called term contract. A faculty member is employed for three or five years. During that period he cannot be removed except for cause. Toward the end of the term contract, he can be reviewed and a decision made as to whether an offer is appropriate for another term contract. In this manner the professional is protected from term to term; and, of course, he must agree each time to any renewal. If all institutions followed this procedure, it is assumed there would be a great deal of interchange and mobility.

Actually, this process would be unnerving and risky for the faculty member. He would be constantly in competition with younger men and women; and at the end of every term he would face the prospect of termination for no cause. For instance, his department head or the administration might change and he would be out for simply personal reasons. Such a system would keep him on his toes but not on his feet. His career would likely always be a little off balance. It is quite unlikely that an institution with term contracts would be able to compete with an institution offering the security of a tenure system. A rolling-term contract (for example three years extension after every year unless notification is given of nonextension) would carry much the same uncertainty, since refusal to extend could occur at the end of any year.

Harvard is sometimes pointed out as the exception that proves that the tenure rules should be changed. Very few obtain tenure at Harvard, and it can take as long as twelve years. Very few expect to attain tenure at Harvard. What they want is the prestige and experience that their time at Harvard will give them in their search for other and more lasting appointments. Not many Harvards can coexist on this level of operation.

Notwithstanding its deficiencies, the trustees should retain the tenure system as the best assurance for academic freedom and economic security.

Probationary Period

What seems clearly indicated is not the abandonment but the strengthening of the tenure system. One very important factor is the length of time of the probationary period. It must be long enough so that the candidate may be constructively helped and evaluated not only for performance but for potential. The National Academic Tenure Commission found that probationary periods varied from two to ten years, excluding the Harvard twelve.

The two-year period is mostly employed at junior colleges. In fact, the "two years," at the most, amounts to eighteen months, because it is established practice to notify a probationer of nonreappointment at least six months before the expiration of his second year. These short probationary periods among the junior colleges derive from their long association with the public schools systems. Many of them emerged from secondary school systems, or maintained administrative ties with them and their original faculty were largely upgraded high school teachers.

But junior or community colleges have been with us for some time, and they have become an essential part of American higher education. The ninety-six junior colleges in California provide open access for the entire secondary school population, and indeed for all persons over eighteen. The junior college movement in other states has been repeating the California experience. Most junior college programs are bifurcated: about half are in the academic area leading into eligibility for transfer to four-year and university institutions; the other half deal with training for a great variety of vocational interests—hotel management, vocational nursing, machine-shop work, and the like. These institutions will be giving postsecondary education to most students.

But the junior colleges cannot be regarded as appendages to the high schools. They do the most vital screening and most important counseling for higher education. They provide the open door for minorities, and their remedial work exceeds in volume and in depth any similar work performed by the senior segments. On the vocational side, their standards have steadily become higher as our technological requirements have increased. As representative institutions of higher education they should be just as careful in the selection of their teaching personnel as any of the senior institutions. For all these reasons, the probationary period of junior college teachers should be extended to at least five years. Recent studies[3] confirm the desirability of a probationary period of approximately seven years in four-year colleges and universities. Such a period affords sufficient time to demonstrate competence and affords a measure of flexibility in planning a table of faculty organization.

Criteria for Evaluation

A faculty member's competence must be evaluated not only in terms of his subject area but in his service to the college—on curriculum committees, personnel committees, and task forces. But his expertise in the subject area comes first. Annual evaluations are important to mark progress, but some anniversaries are more important than others. If the institution has made a serious mistake and this fact is readily apparent, the relationship should be severed immediately at the end of the first year. In the vast number of cases the instructor or assistant professor should be given the benefit of the doubt and carried forward. At the end of the third year and at the end of the fifth year, the evaluations should be particularly detailed. A sufficient time has elapsed and sufficient experience accumulated at these times to indicate the probable future of the probationary member. Moreover, after the fifth year, the reviewing faculty and administration should have a pretty clear idea as to the probability of tenure for the person under consideration. It is only fair procedure that, although the candidate still has the burden to prove his right to tenure, the institution is morally more committed

---

[3] National Commission on Academic Tenure (already cited); and *Report and Recommendations of the Select Committee on the Master Plan for Higher Education,* State of California, 1972.

at the end of the fifth year than it was at the end of the third and that there should be more persuasive reasons for termination.

The question of how evaluation is to be effected is largely professional. The institution can lay down some guide lines in the interests of quality. Research may be an important consideration, but it should not be credited on the basis of the mere quantity of publication. What was published and where and what has been the scholarly reaction are the more critical factors. Teaching performance—the most important aspect in most cases—is in some ways the hardest to measure. Except in cases of team teaching, colleagues do not have much opportunity to observe the candidate. Moreover, the instructor or assistant professor resents the visitation once or twice a term of a senior colleague who may be attending the class on the very day that the candidate is giving an improvised lecture and the visiting professor has indigestion. On the other hand, if the visitation is announced well in advance, the candidate will pull out his best lecture and exaggerate the impression of his capacity. In some institutions, periodic and cooperative visits by several faculty members in the spirit of being helpful rather than critical can improve teaching performance considerably.

The most important factor in the evaluation is probably student input. The students are the clients and over the years they know pretty well whether the professor is stimulating and creative, keeps up with the developments in his field, responds to their needs, and makes his lectures or discussions relevant to their interests. Carefully developed report questionnaires have been put together by various faculties and have proved of considerable assistance in evaluations. Some faculties have commented adversely on student reactions—that students seek out and reward the popular professor, the easy examiner, the giver of good grades. Experience in a number of institutions has proved that this characterization of student opinion is not true. For the most part it has been shown that students prefer a fair but hard grader, a professor who is not superficial and smooth but who treats them as adults and is willing to enter deeply into the complexities of his subject matter. It is true that classes differ and that at times students may go off on a tangent, but over a period of years it can be demonstrated that the best indicator of effective teaching is student evaluation.

Students usually feel that their evaluations are disregarded when faculty committees consider any particular case for retention, tenure, or promotion. It may prove useful if student representatives could appear at a preliminary meeting of the faculty committee and observe that student views are being weighed in the process of review. The student input is an important factor but not necessarily controlling; and it will not serve any useful purpose if students are present during, or participate in, the faculty vote. In other words, it is not proposed that students be the hirers of faculty but simply that their reaction to the teaching performance be clearly understood and considered. If feasible, a supplementary evaluation should be obtained from seniors or graduate students reflecting on their classroom experience three or four years earlier, because there are times when faculty teaching is better appreciated with hindsight.

An institution that desires a strong but equitable tenure policy should establish a table of organization on a department or school basis that, first, provides a ratio of nontenured to tenured spaces and, second, programs employment with age distribution designed to give continuing opportunities to the younger faculty members to attain the tenure spaces. Perhaps the most appropriate relationship is fifty-fifty, but a ratio of sixty tenured positions to forty nontenured reaches a danger point. This is true particularly at a time when, through affirmative action programs, institutions are seeking materially to increase the employment of women and ethnic minority teachers.[4]

If tenured positions become seriously impacted, it may be necessary to hold positions vacant through attrition for a period of time, to extend probationary status temporarily, to employ partly outside of tenure, or to provide term contracts to those for whom tenure is not available.

Trustee policy should strengthen the tenure system by in-

[4] The danger point, according to the National Tenure Commission, ranges from one-half to two-thirds tenured. Some contend that there is no danger point, that a 100 percent tenured faculty would be fully acceptable. But they do not answer the questions relating to financial stringency, closed opportunity for the young and the minorities, and probable loss of quality that such a policy would entail. A phase-in of the tenure ratio may be the fairest procedure (protecting those now on the ladder).

*sisting on an adequate probationary period, diligent reviews of
performance (taking student evaluations as an important factor),
and a ratio of tenured to nontenured faculty that provides opportunity for "new blood."*

Disciplinary Procedures

One area in the tenure system that calls for general improvement is disciplinary procedures. During the period of his appointment
or after tenure is acquired, a faculty member may be dismissed only
for adequate cause and after a fair hearing. Often, adequate cause
is not sufficiently defined, and this deficiency should be remedied.
"Substantial and manifest neglect of duty"; the obligation "to
preserve the dignity and seriousness of university ceremonies and
public exercises"; the obligation "to prevent the disruption or the
effective carrying out of a university function or approved activity
such as lectures, meetings, and public events"—all these examples
set forth prescribed conduct in general but adequate terms.

The burden of proof is upon the institution when it seeks to
discharge for cause. The faculty member is entitled to academic due
process: notice of charges; the opportunity for a fair hearing
and an open hearing, if he prefers it; the right to have counsel and
to cross-examine witnesses.

But due process is not endless process. In recent years many
institutions have found that discharge for cause has become so en-
cumbered with process that it is almost impossible to achieve and
cases are not brought. One committee will be set up to attempt
conciliation, another to bring charges, another to hear the charges,
another to review the recommendations, and another to hear the
appeal after the administrator has made an adverse decision. And in
a multiversity system, there will be a provision for further appeal
beyond the institution itself. This is the machinery of obstruction,
not motion. An institution should provide a simple procedure for
bringing charges, usually by the administration; a single committee
for hearing the charges and making their recommendation to the
president; and possibly the concurrence of the board of trustees if a
discharge is ordered.

Once tenure is granted, it is not easy to obtain evidence of incompetence or of other substantial neglect of duty. Whatever a faculty member's general reputation may be is of little value. Charges must be specific and center on important incidents or events. They must be backed by direct testimony. Moreover, discharge is by no means the only sanction. There can be censure or reprimand, withdrawal of the sabbatical privilege, and suspension with or without pay for a specified period.

The performance of tenured faculty should still be subject to periodic review, say every three to five years. The purpose is not disciplinary but to keep the faculty member alert and aware that performance is still important. Such reviews can affect in-step and merit pay increases or promotions.

The trustees of an institution are ultimately responsible for its tenure policy. They should require their administration and faculty to develop and present a viable tenure policy for adoption by the board. The tests just described may be applied to determine if the policy should be adopted. Since practically all institutions have a tenure policy, what is suggested here is a matter of review and possible amendment. For public institutions, certain aspects of the tenure policy may have to be presented to the state legislature before they can be implemented, especially if the statute itself stipulates the time during which tenure shall be acquired.

Whatever the tenure policy, it should be fully set forth in a handbook and made available to every faculty member. It is only right that a faculty member should be aware of all the conditions of his employment and what is expected and required of him. Disputes are wasteful which arise because no groundwork for mutual understanding has been laid.

From time to time trustees should require reports with respect to the operations of the institution's tenure system: the number of appointments, nonreappointments, and promotions; the number and nature of grievances with respect to nonappointments and promotions and the disposition of them; the same type of information for any disciplinary cases; the status of the policy on the tenure-nontenure ratio; and samples of student evaluations not necessarily identified with the faculty member being evaluated. A board that asks to be informed in these matters will have an affirmative effect on the implementation of policy.

Trustee policy should support simplified, fair disciplinary procedures for dealing with such charges as incompetence, neglect of duty, and unprofessional conduct. The trustees should require periodic reports on how the tenure system is operating.

Appeal Procedures

In some instances the board of trustees may serve as a final board of appeal in faculty disciplinary cases. If the faculty member feels that the faculty committees and the administrative heads, including the president, have dealt unjustly with him, he may then ask the board of trustees to review the entire transcript of his case and hold a special hearing, supplementing this request with a number of letters from friends and colleagues.

However, a board of trustees is not equipped to hear and pass upon this kind of case. The study of a lengthy transcript is a considerable task. A hearing can be escalated into proceedings covering several days or more. A policy-dealing board will be bogged down in this kind of judicial work or give it such superficial attention that none of the appellant's effort will have been worth the time and the energy. Usually, in state procedures there are administrative hearings provided in addition to the academic proceedings, and resort to the courts is always protected in the case of contract violation or the infringement of constitutional rights. It is not essential to add the board to the procedure.

If the board participates in this kind of quasijudicial work, it should do so through a personnel committee consisting of attorney members as well as regular members. If any such consideration is granted, it should be solely on the basis of the record. Occasionally, the trustees will pick up deficiencies in the record which have not been given sufficient weight by the administration. The appropriate penalty may be suspension without pay for a specific period of time rather than discharge. The committee of trustees, in its review and report to the board, may save some time and expense for the interested parties and perhaps avoid an unnecessary investigation by the American Association of University Professors. It is a question whether, considering the priorities, a board has the time to perform this function.

The board may act as a final board of appeal in disciplinary cases involving discharge. It should base its action (of concurrence, reversal, or reduction of penalty) on the record and not hold a new hearing. It should be satisfied that academic due process was followed.

10

FACULTY AND COLLECTIVE BARGAINING

In October 1971, Myron Lieberman published an article in *Harper's* magazine (page 61) entitled "Professors, Unite!" Mr. Lieberman was chairman of the First National Conference on Collective Bargaining in Higher Education in 1970 and is director of Program Development in the office of teacher education at the City University of New York, an institution that has a collective bargaining agreement with its academic employees.

The theme of the article was that collective bargaining for professors had already commenced, that it represented an inevitable development, the wave of the future, and that in the next ten years the colleges and universities in the United States would have "organized" faculties. The professors would be responsive and glad to sign up and actually the whole movement was basically conservative because, Mr. Lieberman said, "unionization and collective bargaining are conservative processes."

The idea that unionization of faculty is inevitable, and therefore all concerned should relax and enjoy it, is heard more and more in the groves of the academy and sometimes in the board rooms of the trustees. However, the claim that any economic or social movement is destined is a familiar technique for spreading the gospel. Almost every political campaign tries to assure the public that the election of its leader is inevitable and you should get on the bandwagon while there is time. The propaganda of manifest destiny or inevitability has the advantage of built-in dynamics; it generates movement because it claims its motor is running.

It is true that collective bargaining has been introduced into a number of institutions of higher education in the eastern part of the United States and more particularly in their junior colleges. Some senior institutions have also been included. The largest institutional prizes for collective bargaining have been won in the State University of New York (with twenty-seven campuses) and in the City University of New York. A number of public institutions in New York, Pennsylvania, Massachusetts, New Jersey, and Michigan also have union contracts.

Still, collective bargaining for faculty does not constitute the pattern for colleges and universities throughout the country, and the process has made relatively small inroads in private universities and colleges. At this juncture, no more than 10 percent of the faculty members are covered by collective bargaining agreements. Both in the public and private institutions the issue of collective bargaining remains one of choice. In a matter of such great importance it should be a conscious choice. If collective bargaining comes to the university or the college, it should be a preferred course of action, not a process that creeps in because a faculty or a system of governance has become resigned to it or has become fatalistic about it.

Causes for Unionization

The historic causes for collective bargaining in industry were related to sweatshop conditions and depressed wages, but, peculiarly enough, the bargaining movement in the academy started during a period of growth, prosperity, and high salaries in the sixties. The unprecedented expansion, employment opportunities, and annual salary increments in higher education made it unlikely that pressures for union organization would arise, but they did. Professors were concerned about their teaching loads, office space, lack of clerical help, supposed unfairness in not being reappointed or promoted, and so on. Conditions of work became more important than salaries and a push for power was more important than either. Also, some felt that the time had come to wrest the power of governance from the trustees and administration.

Many faculty members were not satisfied that their academic senates were acting from positions of strength. They regarded the senates as creatures of the administration—created by it, financed by it, patronized by it. In most cases the senates were advisory bodies—deliberative but not decisive. Those groups that advocated unionization wanted a large share of the decision making in determining the budgets underlying educational policies.

In the seventies economic issues have become more ascendant. Now there is an oversupply of professors desiring employment. Academic funding has become more difficult and in the public areas has had to compete with other social and welfare demands. The lush days of substantial annual increases seem to be over (for the foreseeable future). Indeed, support for the academy has been curtailed—for research, for curriculum, and for salaries and fringe benefits.

The hold of the young professor on his appointment appears less secure during a time of relative austerity. He is afraid that he will be pushed off the tenure ladder for arbitrary reasons. As discussed, tenured positions are becoming impacted in certain institutions, and junior faculty members look upon their narrowing opportunities with concern and alarm. White males feel especially vulnerable because they are caught in the cross fire of affirmative action demands at a time when enrollments are static or regressing. With retrenchment in funding, many faculty members fear that teaching loads will be increased, and some who consider their current load as unduly burdensome feel that it will be maintained.

These considerations affecting the protection of salaries and security furnish a more fertile ground for the seeds of unionization than affluence. That there may be other and perhaps better ways of dealing with these problems is beside the point. Where there are substantive grievances, there will be unions to take advantage of them.

The young faculty demand speedier promotions and benefits, but their concerns also go beyond basic economic issues. The younger faculty are set against both the older tenured faculty and the administration. They are suspicious of merit differentials in pay; they do not like the large federal grant to the distinguished professor who may attempt to build a small academic empire.

In the public institutions, faculty generally fear that the centers of power are moving farther away from them. They believe the trustees are resuming authority that they had once delegated; they see and hear governors, state departments of finance, and legislative bodies declaring and implementing their views about admissions, tuition, employment conditions, teaching load, and curriculum. Thus, they contend that they must organize in order to bring pressure upon more remote centers of power than the administration, which has always been an immediate and ready target.

The junior colleges are a special case. Derived from the secondary school system, many of these colleges were characterized by an authoritarian and bureaucratic regime. The faculty in these institutions found it was difficult to obtain answers to grievances, decisions on curriculum, and to procure money for innovative projects. It was a case of "Up the Down Staircase." The recognition of faculty rights has been slower in these emerging institutions of higher education than in the senior segments. As a result, a number of junior college faculties, recently "graduated" from the school system, have followed the fairly widespread pattern of school teacher unionization.

Private universities and colleges have a different tradition. Many faculty members chose to teach in private institutions because of a belief that they afforded greater flexibility in administration and insulation from many of the periodic fluctuations in attitudes toward public institutions. Moreover, a private institution, particularly a prestigious one, is usually more limited in size and has, in most instances, tried to keep abreast or ahead of public institutions in salaries and in the provision of a pleasant working environment. Nevertheless, private institutions are beginning to feel the impact of bargaining procedures. The National Labor Relations Board has taken jurisdiction over private universities and colleges of any substantial size (those showing a gross revenue in excess of $1 million a year with a substantial portion related to interstate commerce), as demonstrated in the cases of Cornell, Fordham, Adelphi, and Hofstra universities.

Comparison with Industrial Pattern

The term *collective bargaining* is used loosely in the field of higher education. In 1967 the Academic Senate of the California State Colleges conducted a plebescite regarding collective bargaining for these faculties. Five membership organizations—the Association of California State College Professors, the American Federation of Teachers, the California College and University Faculty Association, the California State Employees Association, and the AAUP—gave their respective points of view. They used various phrases, including "collective bargaining," "collective negotiation," and "collective action." The words were not explained in terms of an industrial pattern of collective bargaining or any other. A faculty member is very likely to assume that collective bargaining has the same connotation in higher education as in industry and should function in much the same way. Moreover, the idea of a "collective" approach is appealing. It implies brotherhood, joint action, and strength. But there is considerable difference between collective bargaining in industry and for certain kinds of public institutions as compared with most segments of higher education, as we shall see.

In the California State Colleges, the faculties voted on a statewide basis, and their opinion was about 48 percent for collective bargaining and 52 percent against it. Yet because of the ambiguity of the terminology, no one could be quite certain what the results meant. Since the 1967 vote, it is estimated that a two-thirds majority in the California State Colleges (now the California State University and Colleges) has swung the other way—*for* collective bargaining. But still no one knows precisely whether the individual faculty members prefer any collective bargaining procedure whose principal elements they are all agreed upon.

To understand the possibilities and consequences of collective bargaining, let us examine its anatomy. The fundamental purpose of collective bargaining is to negotiate and settle the terms of a labor contract between an employer on the one side and an organized body of workers on the other. In negotiating and administering the contract, the employer deals with the organization as the exclusive representative of the workers or employees. The employer does not deal with the employees in other groups or individually. The following additional factors should be noted:

The collective bargaining agreement is between parties having the capacity to bargain. Each party must be able to carry out the obligations of the agreement reached.

The line between employer and employee is clearly drawn. Personnel who have supervisory functions or who are involved in determining management policy are excluded from the employees' bargaining unit. By the same token, employees are excluded from most of the decision-making authority reserved to management. Management has broad reserved authority, either expressed or implied: it schedules operations and determines production or distribution policy; it has the right to discharge for cause, subject to a grievance procedure administered by a committee in which management shares membership equally with the representatives of the labor organization and, in case of a deadlock, most contracts provide that an impartial arbitrator determines the validity of the discharge. The provision for arbitration can also apply to other disputes under the contract.

The exclusive bargaining agent represents an appropriate employee unit of the employer. The unit has common interests in relation to its own members and to the employer. A single negotiation and contract may cover a number of plants in an extended area if the interests and needs are substantially the same.

The subjects of bargaining are generally wages, hours, and working conditions. Working conditions are often defined in broad terms. Similarly, vacation rights, sick leave, holidays, pension benefits, and many other factors with a cost tag are included. The contract is mostly concerned with economic items.

Negotiations are usually conducted in secret until the point of agreement or impasse. In extensive operations involving a large number of employees, both sides are usually represented by experienced negotiators. Negotiations are conducted at arm's length. It is essentially an adversary process during the bargaining period and has been so characterized by the United States Supreme Court and in articles written by faculty members discussing the potentials of collective bargaining in the colleges. The president of Local 2 of the United Federation of Teachers, New York City, described collective bargaining negotiations as a state of war, where maximum pressures are brought to bear and where both sides must stay on a war footing.

The demands, claims, tactics, and actions of collective bargaining are quite different from the modes of expression and techniques usually employed by the academic process in efforts to present materials, opposing views, and solutions.

The employer pays his own bargaining costs and the bargaining agent pays his own costs; these include costs of representation, travel expenses, if necessary, and of accumulation and development of data and information.

In the event of an impasse, each side reserves the right to use sanctions to persuade or compel the other side to agree to its position. The employer must risk the loss of profit, the employees the loss of pay, in seeking their objectives. The ultimate sanction is the strike in the case of employees and a lockout in the case of employers. The right to strike has been described as essential to collective bargaining.

A number of distinctions exist when the factors noted are applied to a public system of education that has no taxing power:

It is clear that most trustees of state universities and colleges are not in the position to enter into a binding contract with any labor organization covering any matter that will cost the state money. The trustees could not obligate themselves to spend because, in the main, they can spend only the money they receive from legislative appropriations. With no taxing power, they do not have the same authority as boards of supervisors or district school boards or, on occasion, junior college district boards, which do have the power to set tax rates. The trustees of private universities and colleges and a few autonomous senior public institutions can, within economic limits, set tuition rates and legally may be in a more realistic position to bargain.

Other agencies outside of the trustees of a four-year or graduate public institution have considerable authority in budgetary matters—the state department of finance, the governor in most instances, and the legislature. Faculty organizations in California have recommended that these other agencies, executive and legislative, be made parties to an agreement, but there has been no indication that any of these agencies would participate in such a procedure. From the legislative standpoint, it would seem impractical and contrary to the doctrine of legislative independence. No committee of the legislature could bind the entire legislature; the legislature holds hearings before it enacts legislation; it does not bargain with any special interest group or segment to make a contract binding upon itself.

It is quite apparent from the point just made that the trustees do not have the independent capacity to bargain. But the trustees can be given the power subject to approval by the other agencies of government and the legislature. This procedure has been followed in the New York Taylor Act and in the Michigan Public Employment Relations Act. It is still an open question in Michigan whether the statute applies to the faculties in higher education, particularly those of the constitutional agencies such as the University of Michigan and Michigan State University. (The issue is moot at Michigan State University since the faculty rejected collective bargaining by a two to one vote.[1]) In New York, if the education administration fails to reach agreement with the union or the governor's office (the latter seems to bear the burden of bargaining), a series of steps is provided to break the impasse, including fact finding and mediation by legislative committees, and all procedures must be completed by a specified date prior to final budget hearings. Ultimately, the legislature determines the budget. Thus, the collective

[1] However the Assembly Advisory Council on Public Employee Relations (a citizens committee) has advised the California State Assembly that a general public employees statute on collective bargaining would apply to the constitutional agency of the University of California.

bargaining is somewhat illusory since the legislature must make the final decision as it does in the case of any appropriation.

The New York and Michigan statutes declare that all public employees, including faculty, do not have the right to strike. This was the *quid pro quo* for authorizing the collective bargaining pattern. Yet the public school teachers in New York participated in a long strike despite the provisions of the Taylor Act, their union president went to jail, a heavy fine was imposed, and the teachers received an increase in pay in the settlement which easily wiped out the penalty of the fine. In Michigan, despite the no-strike provision, strikes have been common in the public schools, and one of the colleges was shut down by a faculty strike. In short, the no-strike provision was inadequately enforced or possibly it could not be effectively enforced.

This analysis has been set forth to indicate that collective bargaining in higher education, certainly in public higher education, cannot and does not follow an industrial pattern. A further observation may be made, namely, that when statutory authorization is given permitting collective bargaining or an adaptation of it, the very fact that such authorization exists is a great stimulus to collective bargaining. The legislature can turn on the faucet.

Effect on Institutional Relationships

Collective bargaining (even in an adapted form) will change the relationship between the institution and the faculty. The traditional academic structure has been one of shared responsibility. True, final authority has rested with the trustees, but, as a practical matter, a vast amount of authority has been delegated to administration and to the faculty itself. Most questions on faculty status—appointment, promotion, and tenure—are within the area of faculty control, as are curriculum and other matters affecting the educational process, including relations with students. Faculty senates, though created or authorized by the trustees, work with them and advise with them in varying degrees of cooperation; boards of trustees that make a habit of disregarding faculty counsel are rare and headed for controversy. The theory of traditional arrangements is that the academy is a joint enterprise, independent to a considerable extent, and based upon a shared responsibility and loyalty to the institution and a shared commitment to the same purposes and values.

When economic matters and issues of governance are subject to negotiation, the relationships become formalized and adversary. This may not be the intention of either party, but parties with opposing positions cannot meet to resolve their differences without engaging in adversary proceedings.

Access of faculty to the president and to the trustees, under the traditional form of governance, is frequently informal. Top policy makers become more remote when detailed contracts must be negotiated.

Faculty senates are likely to be weakened or wither away before the more aggressive claims of the collective bargaining organizations. Again, this may not be the intention, but the scope of collective bargaining usually enlarges upon itself, and though limited to economic issues at the beginning, it will soon engulf collateral and educational programs. The union will either bypass the senate or dominate it.[2]

Under collective bargaining, the individual faculty member will also find himself more remote from the centers of influence and authority, for he will have delegated representation to his bargaining agent. He will find that, except through his agent, his voice may not be heard and even the agent may not hear the voice of the traditional faculty member if the agent owes his election to junior faculty. (Recently an election was held at the University of Hawaii, and the American Federation of Teachers was selected as agent over the AAUP. The reason was that the faculty in the junior college branches voted for the AFT, while the fewer senior faculty of the main institution in Honolulu voted for the AAUP or no agent. This

----

[2] Of interest here is the fact the American Association of University Professors, which is not a union in the usual sense, has developed what they consider to be an educational model for collective bargaining. It is their position, in selected situations, to enter the bargaining contest with the purpose of buttressing, by contract, the rights of the academic senate and traditional faculty prerogatives and procedures. If bargaining must come, this alternative may be preferred by trustees, but the AAUP would first have to win the representation in election.

situation shows how important the appropriate unit, statewide or local, may be in an election and the different interests of faculty within the same unit.)

By the same token, administrators become more management conscious. The faculty are viewed as employees, the administration as management. The concept of "we" and "they" is crystallized.

It can be expected that the trend toward placing faculty members on boards of trustees will also be reversed. Faculty cannot be on both sides of the bargaining table (even faculty from other institutions; if they are of the same or of a different union, they may have a conflict). Similarly, trustees might find it less compatible with their management function to include faculty members on their committees to select a president or to approve high administrative appointments.

Collective bargaining can be very costly in time, effort, and money. The trustees cannot engage in it and it would be unwise for the administration to assign its chief officers to negotiate. Yet administrators who thoroughly understand the academic scene must participate in the negotiations or oversee them in order to protect the interests of the institution. The chief negotiators, however, should be specially employed for their expertise in negotiation and their knowledge of personnel and labor practices. Obviously, they may be drawn from persons who have been active in university affairs in an administrative capacity or as arbitrators in industrial disputes; the main point is that they be knowledgeable and skilled.

Collective bargaining in the field of higher education has shown an egalitarian bias. It is against pay differentials, particularly merit pay. It is against special awards to faculty members. It wants all treated alike for the purposes of seniority, increases in pay, and working conditions. It seeks a competent, but homogenized, faculty. The quality in higher education may be strained out through such a leveling process.

Also, there is the question of union procedure. Ordinarily, a union reports its demands and negotiations in excessive terms, trusting to win benefits through final adjustments and compromises. It reports background conditions and considerations in a rather one-sided manner. Industrial management, which does considerable puffing of its own in its advertising, understands this technique. The process is quite alien to professors engaged in the search for truth and dedicated to testing their theories and positions by objective standards. The strong language of union claims and demands upset them. What is likely to happen is that the professor who tries to maintain his intellectual integrity inside and outside the classroom abandons his interest and participation in collective bargaining. In turning his back on the process, he simply frees the bargaining agents to go about their business in the customary way. Moreover, the academic profession is highly individualistic, and collective action in which all speak with a single voice goes against the grain.

This may be an idealization of the matter. The younger faculty and the politician professors—those more interested in governance—are more inclined to fight fire with fire and to forget the standards of their intellectual pursuits when they contend for higher salaries and more comfortable working arrangements. I recall the complaint of the representative of one academic organization who was protesting to the trustees of the California State Colleges about financial controls imposed by the chancellor upon the individual colleges. He argued: "We are oppressed; it is like living in a concentration camp." My mind went back to the time when I saw a Nazi concentration camp immediately after its liberation toward the end of World War II. I saw those skeletal people and looked again at this ardent, well-fed, comfortable professor. His rhetoric appeared more political than academic.

Up to this point, there is a good deal of controversy as to whether collective bargaining in higher education has produced any startling results, whether, except for a few instances, the pay scales in the senior segments of higher education have been raised any higher than they would have been under the traditional legislative process. The greatest success has been achieved in the junior colleges and in the lower ranks of professors, where pay scales have been substantially raised. Collective bargaining has not come to the junior colleges in California because they are controlled by the Winton Act, which provides for a joint organizational council and conference type of relationship with the governing district—and not for the bargaining process.

There are, of course, some strong arguments for instituting collective bargaining in higher education. The union seeks to test prevailing forms and conditions at every turn and compels an institution to examine and reexamine its operations. Administration learns more about its problems and programs through an intense bargaining session than it would in the normal course of periodic self-analyses. There tends to be a simplification of relationships between trustees and administration on the one hand and faculty on the other. Sometimes it is easier to deal with employees than with partners. The administration loses some of its tensions because the final unpleasant decisions are referred to the political centers.

But as yet there is no comparison of faculty benefits won through traditional procedures and through collective bargaining. Somehow the flexible, informal arrangements developed through academic custom and practice have provided a professional life that is unique in its independence and desirability as compared with almost any other form of professional or vocational activity. Certain of these freedoms go back to medieval times. They should not be casually transferred or abandoned.

There are viable alternatives to collective bargaining. One is to support and strengthen the academic senates. This can be done in various ways:

First, the trustees can expressly delegate certain functions such as control of curriculum and faculty status in all normal circumstances, reserving only minimum rights to modify or veto in exceptional cases involving institutional survival or integrity, or

Second, they can widen the scope of consultation (that is, the serious exchange of views) to include fiscal as well as educational policy, and, particularly in matters of educational and faculty status, they can follow the counsel of the senate except in rare and unusual circumstances.

Third, the trustees can allow the faculty membership organizations significant participation in the development of fiscal policies. The most logical way is for these organizations to make their proposals to the academic senate so that they may be fully evaluated before recommendations are made to the administration and the trustees. If this procedure does not satisfy the membership organizations, the administration should confer periodically with them so as to procure and exchange views. However, the administration should make no commitments until the senate makes its report.

Membership organizations can also be constituted into a council for the sole purpose of dealing with economic matters along with representatives of the academic senate. Before a proposed budget is adopted, the council will have its opportunity to meet with the administration in an effort to bring about a consensus on all points possible. This concept of a council is used in the public schools in California under the authority of statute. Its advantage is that it consolidates and centralizes discussions so that issues are brought into sharp focus with all faculty parties present. However, an unsolved problem of this procedure is that the American Federation of Teachers sometimes refuses to participate in such a council because it believes the council subverts or deflects the principles of unionization and across-the-table bargaining.

Fourth, give to faculty a significant voice in the selection of the president. This means that the trustee selection committee should include faculty representatives who will participate fully with the other members in recommending the final candidates to the trustees. It should be unusual for such a committee to recommend a candidate opposed by all the faculty representatives.

Position of Trustees

Whatever the merits of the contentions, the issue of collective bargaining will be presented to many institutions, public and private, during the seventies. Confronted with this issue, what should a board of trustees do?

The trustees should study the facts as they pertain to their institution. They should understand what collective bargaining may mean for their campus or group of campuses. The Trustees of the California State Colleges studied the matter for more than a year before taking a position in 1966–67. They investigated the legalities and the merits; authorized their Faculty and Staff Affairs Committee to investigate the question and bring in recommendations; held two long hearings to which all of the membership organizations, including the American Federation of Teachers, contributed; and considered a majority and a minority report. After much discussion, the trustees resolved against the collective bargaining concept. Of course, conditions can change for any institution. The state legislature may authorize collective bargaining for public employees, including academic employees, in which case the faculty of a public institution can insist that a collective bargaining agent be recognized. In the private institution of any substantial size, 30 percent of the faculty can compel an election under National Labor Relations Board auspices.

If the first order of business is for the trustees to understand the subject, the second is to be as certain as they can that faculty members know what they are considering when they are debating the issue of collective bargaining. The faculty senate should be the chief agency to encourage thorough investigation, report, and evaluation. Trustees should be certain that the faculty understands the alternatives available and the advantages and disadvantages of each. The faculty senate itself should be asked (although usually this will not be necessary) to analyze its own position and prospects in a system of collective bargaining. Will it have a function? Will it be attenuated? What are the short- and long-term probabilities?

The board should declare its position. Naturally many faculty members will regard it as the self-serving position of an employer. But the trustees are the legal governors and they should take leadership in expressing their views concerning what they believe to be in the best interests of the institution. It is common practice for the employer in National Labor Relations Board elections to give his position to employees, and it is similarly in order in the education field.

This is particularly true if the legislature has not yet established authority for collective bargaining. The governor and the legislature are entitled to know the trustees' attitude and their reasons. The future of collective bargaining for academic employees may be in the hands of the legislature, because if no statutory authority is is extended, collective bargaining can not be implemented. Moreover, even if the legislature is inclined to authorize some form of collective bargaining to cover the rank and file of public employees, it does not follow that it will necessarily extend such authorization to the academic area. For many years the academy has had its own form of academic input, participation, and discipline and can properly be excluded from a general statute.[8]

---

[8] The Assembly Advisory Council (California), referred to in foot-

In all probability the New York collective bargaining law would not have been applied to higher education if the academic authorities had been sufficiently alerted to the prospect of its inclusion; because until the last moment, it was thought that higher education was excluded. Public trustees must keep abreast of important legislative developments in this field.

If collective bargaining comes to their institution, the trustees should do everything possible to help establish a sensible legal structure. Industrial collective bargaining patterns simply will not apply in the public field for most senior institutions since, as noted, the final decisions are made within the legislative process. Therefore, the executive branches (the governor and the finance department) should be brought together with the trustees in the bargaining procedure so that when tentative arrangements are made they will at least have executive approval. If there is an impasse in negotiations, then legislative fact-finding should occur early enough in the budgetary process so that all parties have time to make their positions known and to support them.

With all this opportunity to make and reply to demands and determine the facts, strikes and lockouts should be prohibited, as in the case of the New York Taylor Act. The continuation of mass education without interruption is vital to the welfare of the community. Strikes and picketing are bitter pills for most faculty to swallow, and they embitter poststrike relationships as in no other community. But if after the legislative process is completed, a strike nevertheless occurs, the trustees should seek to invoke statutory penalties and other legal procedures to protect the institution. They should seek an injunction (if one may be obtained under the law) only if they fully intend to use it. Violators of injunctions (usually for manning an unlawful picket line) are subject to imprisonment for contempt, and most faculty members have no conception of jail or punishment by confinement. But, if contempt proceedings are

---

note 1 of this chapter, stated that it was unfair to omit higher education faculties in public-employee collective-bargaining coverage. The council concluded that faculties should not be denied the choice of union versus traditional forms. Assuming statutory authorization, it would be a more informed choice if faculty advocates of the traditional form were as well financed as union organizers.

enforced, jail may be their resting place. This is an unhappy end, even to contention.[4]

If unionization comes, the trustees should direct their representatives to do everything possible to exclude educational policy (including academic freedom questions) and the disciplinary and grievance procedures from the scope of collective bargaining. This has been done in several of the bargaining contracts in New York and Michigan. Then collective bargaining deals with economic issues, and academic matters continue to be reserved to the academic community, unless a faculty member selects the union to represent him in a disciplinary or grievance case. The exclusions described should be fought for, but initial success should not blind the trustees to the ultimate prospects. The first contract and occasionally the second are sometimes known in industry as sweetheart contracts. But the long-term goals of the union are to expand the scope of bargainable subjects.[5] The challenge to the trustee is to conserve the traditional academic forms and procedures as long as possible.[6]

Some unions claim that academic freedom is better supported when it becomes part of an enforceable union contract. Most faculty would regard the placement of such an essential matter on a term

[4] Some authorities believe that when prolonged mediation and fact-finding efforts have failed, the public employer should have the right to lock out and the union to strike after a period of five to ten days, provided that within that time the public employer, union, or any citizen who would be affected by the interruption of service be permitted to file for injunctive relief to prevent the strike or lock out. The court would be empowered to grant an injunction only when the strike or lock-out imminently threatens public health or safety, a situation that could, but would not be likely to, obtain in a strike against the academy.

[5] Admittedly working conditions and educational policy occasionally overlap, as in the case of class size.

Putting the grievance and disciplinary procedures under the usual collective bargaining process takes a multitude of academic forms and practices (including tenure) outside the academic forum and exposes them to third-party arbitration in the labor-management field. Professional arbitrators will make the decisions rather than promotion, tenure, and disciplinary committees.

[6] If the sole contract objective of the union is to establish these forms in an agreement, the trustees might modify their approach regarding the exclusion of all but economic issues. Then the economic issues would also be subordinated to the traditional forms.

contract basis to be a step backward. To include academic freedom suggests that it is negotiable and expires when the contract ends. The right is so fundamental that its inclusion is probably immaterial.

If collective bargaining is established, the trustees must seriously consider modifications in institutional practices in order to clarify the management function. For example, in many institutions faculty representatives participate in the selection of the president and other high academic officials. In a system of collective bargaining, should the top executive be selected in part by his employees? The initial impulse, as previously indicated, is to say no; but it may prove better for the development of sound bargaining relations and the exclusion of academic matters if certain of the established procedures with the Senate are retained. A president who is selected independently of any faculty consultation may find that he is handicapped. However, if academic matters are included in bargaining or if there is a likelihood of union control of faculty participation, it does not appear that faculty consultation with respect to a presidential appointment is warranted.

In any event, campus faculty members should not be included on the board of trustees. There are times when a board must meet to determine interim or final collective bargaining positions, and these, of course, should not be shared with the opposing party. The position of a noncampus faculty member should be carefully considered in his interest as well as that of the institution.

Finally, the board of trustees should authorize the employment of skilled and capable negotiators. Bargaining is no place for amateurs on either side. Experienced negotiators will not lead the institution into needless confrontations. A measure of impersonality and remoteness is introduced in the collective bargaining system, but that is the nature of the process. Although I believe that collective bargaining is not the best procedure for academic institutions, that it is not the wave of the future unless it is passively accepted and more feasible alternatives abandoned, that changes in board structure and reforms in procedure will accomplish more for higher education and the maintenance of its quality—I believe that higher education can live with it and adapt to it.

Trustees should study the causes of the collective bargaining movement for faculty and the implications of such bargaining for their institution. If they decide to oppose it, then as a matter of principle they should declare their position and their reasons to the faculty and in relation to any pending legislation.

If trustees are to provide an alternative to collective bargaining, they should effectively include faculty in the decision-making process, if necessary by expanding areas of delegation of authority and consultation with faculty.

If collective bargaining comes to their institution, the trustees should do everything possible to ensure a viable adaptation of the process. Usually they should limit the bargaining to economic issues. They will find it necessary to exclude campus faculty participation (if it exists) on the board. They will require the administration to employ experienced negotiators.

11

UNDERSTANDING
STUDENTS

The principal purpose of colleges and universities is to teach students. The success or failure of higher education is to be measured by its effect on students. The billions of dollars spent on physical plant, on faculty salaries, on dormitories, on research related to instruction come to very little if the students reject the educational program. In a sense, they are the consumers of the educational product; the consumer is not always right, but he is certainly the chief object of the producer's concern; and trustees must never forget that their institution exists to serve students.

In the sixties, when student restlessness and unhappiness broke out frequently into protest and violence, their acts discouraged and disillusioned the public and on numerous occasions brought about violent and tragic reaction. Then came Kent State and Jackson State and a kind of explosion that shook the country to some measure of sober thought. President Nixon in 1970 appointed the Commission on Campus Unrest, under the chairmanship of William W. Scranton, which produced a controversial report. Many

154

officials thought the report condoned permissiveness, others that it produced new, compelling insights that must be heeded in dealing with students now and in the future.

Most important, it focused not just on stopping violence but on determining its causes. In doing so it went beyond the more familiar causes for unrest—opposition to the Indochina war, racism, and the universities' complicity and internal deficiencies. The report found that the young had developed a new youth culture that undergirded most of their protest. Although only a few students conducted themselves according to the principles of this culture, there was a great deal of sympathy for much of it from the student body as a whole.

While it was admitted that generalizations, as always, are hazardous, certain elements of protest were common. The students rejected their parents' world and attitude toward values. They did not believe in accumulating material things. They had no faith or trust in reason. They opposed the burdensome complexities of civilization which seemed to destroy the joy of living. They wanted to return to the simple life; they wanted to live it to the fullest, and they did not believe regular, disciplined hard work would enable them to do it.

Most of the ideas of the modern student were gleaned from affluent and liberal parents. At home the young people learned that social justice and compassion were the primary values and that there was something fundamentally wrong in the rat race of everyday work and living. The parents often failed to convey that their own comfort usually resulted from hard work and self-discipline.

Whether they did or not, the students took their parents at their word and decided to live the values their parents talked about. If you believe in peace, you must stop war. If you believe in justice, you must open up opportunity to all ethnic groups. If you believe in the simple life, you must reject most of the world's goods. If you believe in down-to-earth solutions, you must oppose complicated corporate structures. If you believe in pleasure, you must keep work at a minimum. If you are against the rich, you must identify with the poor.

And what about the university? If the university is associated with values you detest, you must protest against the university. If the industrial and business worlds are cold and impersonal and the larger universities demonstrate the same features, you must contend against them. If the university is associated with war research, you must strike it down. If it seeks to impose intellectual discipline by specifying too many requirements for admissions, for majors, for degrees, you must protest it. If the university authorities appeal to reason and experience, you must refuse to concede, because truth is not reason—it is instinctive, emotional, and free. In other words, you are against the establishment. Your father and mother were right, they simply failed to live up to their principles.

Now this exposition is a rather free and certainly incomplete interpretation of some of the observations contained in the Scranton commission's report. In a few instances I may have drawn the lines more sharply than the report itself, but the essentials seem to be there.

Since the end of the sixties there has been comparative calm on the campus. Another generation of students seems to have taken over. Some observers believe that a new malaise has descended, a return to the apathy of the fifties. Others credit today's students with a realistic and pragmatic approach to campus life: they want an education that will lead to jobs and security. They note that the charismatic student leaders of the past decade have all but disappeared. The Vietnam war is no longer a call to protest. Students have participated widely in the election process. International tensions have been somewhat relieved. The world may still be out of joint, but it is apparently livable.

Moreover, students have learned that the university is not so vulnerable when the community rallies to its support. In a long, drawn-out battle the police and the establishment will win. Jail sentences are unpleasant and records of conviction do not help a student to enter the mainstream of economic and political life.

Yet it would be a mistake to think that youth has lost its skepticism or capability for anger. Third-world students will continue to fight for educational opportunity and expanded admissions; severe cutoffs of public aid will bring protest and reaction; heavy increases in tuition and other education costs will stimulate strong counterpressures. An American military adventure in any part of the world, an exposure of hypocrisy in nuclear arms control, a defeatist approach to saving the cities—any of these developments could alarm students sufficiently to make them believe that survival was at stake and the campus would again be in turmoil. Youth has not suddenly become optimistic or converted to the support of the status quo (their cynicism has been whetted by Watergate). They are simply more practical, more cautious. They will avoid confrontations until they feel threatened or desperate.

In the seventies, there has been comparative calm on the campuses, and students tend to want an education that will lead to jobs and security, but trustees should not assume that students have lost the skepticism or capacity for anger that undergirded the protests of the sixties.

Approach to Youth

One of the great missions of higher education in the seventies should be to reach the students. Out of a more honest communication will come a better society. But the trustees have a double problem: even if a board is restructured, the trustees will always be regarded as the establishment. They are too few to contact the students effectively. The main contact must be made through the faculty, a secondary contact may be made through the community. The important point is that the contact must be made and the university mission better defined and implemented, or mass higher education may become wasteful and almost destructive of itself and society. With mass higher education becoming a fact of life, the new society is being formed in our colleges and universities. Trustees must be part of the academic coalition that will make the college and university experience constructive for society.

The necessary approach to youth is a frank appraisal of their strengths and their weaknesses. Unquestionably the youth of the sixties made an unprecedented impact on American history. They either led or greatly accelerated American disapproval of the Vietnam war and were largely responsible for the reversal of government policy. This is no little achievement.

Youth has given solid evidence of its commitment to making this a better world—more equal in opportunity, more reflective of the social obligations of industry, more environmentally pure. They have worked in the Peace Corps and antipoverty programs, in tutorial work for disadvantaged students, in efforts to control and relieve pollution, in the civil rights movement.

Youth has also challenged our consumer-oriented society. Is the challenge wrong? Look at your television set. When the lady saves her marriage by serving one kind of coffee; when a housewife becomes delirious over a new detergent; when romance depends upon two sets of teeth gleaming at each other—we have overdone it. We have become overwhelmed by the hard sell of the soft mattress. And American overuse of the resources of the earth itself represents a danger to all mankind. Many members of the establishment can agree with these criticisms. On the basis of such agreement the beginnings of an understanding with youth can be achieved.

Of course youth cannot be fitted into any single category any more than any other people. There are conservative and conformist youth, leftists, hippies, quiet ones, noisy protesters, achievers. Indeed youth in the upper levels of achievement in undergraduate and graduate programs demonstrate an intellectual capacity that is almost unprecedented; they are the brighest students of recent times.

Nevertheless, certain cultural carryovers from the sixties underlie the attitudes of many youth; some of these carryovers (like the emphasis on human and environmental values) are most creditable and spell hope for the future, but some are still negative and seem at odds with the objectives of the university and the building of a better society. These latter views against certain established values and conditions offer challenges to higher education.

To begin with there is the apparent repudiation of our heritage. To many youth, the world seems to have begun in the fifties. There is no past worth studying, no lessons of history to be learned. The only important matters are current ones; the then should be forgotten, the now must be lived. But even if some youth would like to return to nature, they should find out how man once existed in a state of nature. If some youth want to reform the country, they should know the history of the country. History is one of the core subjects of a liberal education. Only when man goes to his own record does he understand himself, know his errors, gain hope for his achievements and his potential. The university should strongly encourage the study of history.

A second attitude for concern is the general opposition to reason, which is an opposition to the fundamental purposes of the university as we have known it. You may be motivated to pursue truth by your heart, but if you grasp it at all, it will be with your mind. Unless all ideas are freely exchanged and examined, you will not be able to test them, weigh them, or evaluate them. If higher education permits antirationalism to dominate its teaching, it is no longer higher education. On this issue the university must take its stand. A student who is not willing to examine human and social problems with *reason* is not qualified as a university student. If he continues to repudiate reason, for example, if he claps and makes a racket in order to prevent his professor from discussing a viewpoint which the student does not approve, he should be excluded from the class and, upon repetition, from the university.

A related cultural attitude is a lack of respect for disciplined study. Too many students believe that they can learn simply by exchanging conversation in informal groups and encounters. Certainly there is great value in the college bull session, currently called rapping, but it is no substitute for hard reading, writing, and analysis. Many students also prefer to avoid any quantitative measurement of their knowledge or progress; they do not like examinations. All of us know that some examinations are unfair either in their questions or their grading; but, by and large, examinations require concentration and study under pressure. The value of the examination is mostly in the preparation for it. Later students will find that they are evaluated all of their lives—the doctor will lose a patient; the lawyer will lose a client; the auto mechanic will lose a customer if he fails to deliver a quality grade of service. In the world outside the campus, performance is the test. And on the campus, the more theoretical examination is the test. Learning is not necessarily enjoyment; thinking may be a painful process, but disciplined study, however disagreeable it may be from time to time, is the prerequisite for a knowledgeable, educated person.

A fourth cultural attitude has its plusses and minuses. The effort to live a simpler life is worthy and desirable; we could eliminate a vast number of gadgets and be happier. But youth goes beyond attacking gadgetry; it fails to recognize the complexities of modern civilization. We are an urbanized and interdependent society. As we go about our everyday business, we forget the vast number of pipes and lines that are under and over our streets, the sources of power deep in the mountains, the spidery network of millions of parts that constitute our telephone and communications systems. We forget that airplanes were not hatched from eggs, and we take light and power and water and food and houses for granted. Only when the power suddenly goes off and office workers are stalled on the fiftieth floor of a skyscraper do we understand how vulnerable and sensitive our urban society can be. It is a very intricate and complicated watch put together over a thousand years. Youth would like to simplify it, but they cannot. They were brought into the twentieth century, not into the first. We are dealing with mass housing, mass production, mass transit, mass education, not with a few people in the meadow. Youth must understand the complexities and benefits of urban civilization, else they will not be able to carry it on. Higher education cannot fulfill its function if it permits the students to shut their minds to this complexity.

And, finally, many youth lack a sense of humor, which means a sense of perspective. Too many of our college youth are rather stuffy, rigid, and conformist in their nonconformity. The American has always seen the funny side of things. He has always seen his fellow man as something less than perfect—the teacher, the preacher, the politician. Much of American humor is directed against the stuffiness and rigidity of people. The puritan ethic has always been with us, but we have always suspected the puritan.

What do these considerations portend for university policy? Only this: that the university must not give up certain inalienable principles. To remain a university it must insist that its intellectual climate be one of reason, require disciplined study, inculcate some understanding of the history of mankind and the complexities of urban civilization, and be unyielding in the pursuit of truth and in the right and duty to pursue truth through many avenues and perspectives. To help preserve these values is part of the trust of trustees. They may allow or encourage a variety of teaching methods, different ways of organizing and presenting the curriculum, changes in admission requirements, innovation in curriculum and procedures, shorter periods of matriculation, and many kinds of graduate degrees. But on the fundamentals of what makes a university, there must be no compromise.

Trustees should recognize the positive contributions and exceptional abilities and potential of a great many present-day students. The trustees should also be aware that youth carries over some of its negative approaches to history, reason, disciplined study, the complexity of modern civilization, and perspective. These latter attitudes constitute challenges to higher education.

Student Conduct

Nothing I have said should be construed as a wish to inhibit student independence of thought or the right to dissent. Exposure to the marketplace of ideas does not mean that the customers will buy the same ideas. Dissent, especially from youth, is to be expected. There can be no improvement without dissent.

But dissent concerns the right to disagree, to express contrary opinions, and to act to put them into effect in lawful ways. Rallies or assemblies protesting war or industrial pollution or the discharge of an unpopular professor are perfectly in order. This attitude has been so uniformly expressed throughout higher education, and by major public figures from both political parties, that it does not merit any further elaboration. There is a fraction of alienated youth (less than previously) so one-sided, so committed, so ruthless, that it believes our present society, including the university, must be destroyed. These youths are willing to enlist support from street people, high school students, or militant adult groups to accomplish their revolutionary objectives. They do not have a positive program —theirs is a burning nihilism. These young people are too angry to conciliate, too resistant to teach, too dangerous to permit to remain. They should be identified, isolated, and excluded.

Fortunately, this is easier to accomplish in the seventies than it was during the turbulent sixties, mainly because most students now understand that if the institution is torn down they will not receive an education. Accordingly, it is now more difficult to capture the cooperation of the liberal-minded students if the objective is to be pursued violently. Moreover, there is a growing understanding that youth may accomplish change within the system. Thousands upon thousands are engaged in political activity. The votes of millions are being counted—new voters from eighteen upward. They sense participation and power. With the acquisition of responsibilities in line with their adult status, they may help to make the world a better place. What they do and how they do it may affect the politics of the world.

Higher education was ill prepared to deal with student revolt between 1964 and 1970. During that period colleges and universities learned a great deal about the rights and responsibilities of students. They found, for instance, that it is unlawful to expel a student without making charges against him and without giving him a hearing. But, in addition, they found that the courts will uphold those decisions that are made after fair hearings on campus. The hearings need not reproduce the process of a criminal trial; nor does the weight of evidence have to be beyond a reasonable doubt, as in a criminal trial—substantial evidence will suffice. Moreover, there is no double jeopardy in bringing a student to trial for purposes of student discipline *before* a criminal trial involving the same alleged acts. In short, higher education can act if it wills to do so. And experience seems to show that the offending student fears a long-time suspension or expulsion much more than jail for a misdemeanor. If college and university administrators act firmly and fairly to clean their own house, they will be successful.

But to be fair, the student should be notified as to what kind of conduct is expected of him in the university or college and what kind of penalties can result if the conduct is breached. Like the faculty handbook, there should be a student handbook of rights and responsibilities developed for every institution. The requirements for student behavior may be of a higher order than commonly prevails in the community outside of the campus. Conduct that causes the disruption of the educational process may not in itself be a crime. Such a statement of rights and responsibilities is best prepared with the cooperation of representative students. Except for those on the militant fringes, the students will usually participate in the drafting of appropriate regulations.

Wherever feasible, students should be well represented on

disciplinary committees in order to contribute peer understanding to disciplinary proceedings; but they should not be in a position of control—the exposure to peer pressure would simply be too great.

Fact finding, however, is usually better done by some experienced outside person, such as an attorney, judge, or trained hearing officer. The committee should review the facts as found by the hearing officer and recommend the appropriate disciplinary action to the administration, but the president of the university or the college should have the final decision. The trustees normally should not intervene in a student disciplinary case.

Trustees should be assured that students receive a statement of rights and responsibilities in whose preparation students have participated.

Trustee policy should provide fair, uncomplicated hearings for serious student disciplinary cases, preferably using an outside hearing officer to determine facts.

Police on Campus

Trustees should adopt clear policies regarding bringing police on campus. It is better, of course, to consider these policies, if they are not already in effect, at a time of comparative calm than at a time of emergency.

The question is not whether police may be permitted to enter a campus and enforce the law. They have the general duty to enforce the law. If they have reasonable cause to believe that a crime is about to be committed or that the danger of injury to person or property is imminent, they may insist on being present and taking such lawful action as they deem necessary. Some public officials have argued that since the police are responsible for law and order, they themselves should be ever watchful of campus conditions and perform their duty without request or invitation.

However, experience has shown that the presence of uniformed police often has the effect of stimulating or escalating mob activity rather than of deflating it. It seems to be an American reflex to be resistant to the policeman. The driver stopped for going through a red signal or exceeding the speed limit usually thinks of at least three different reasons why it is a dirty trick for the policeman

to give him a ticket. Any mass of people requested to stand behind a
rope in order to watch a parade will react angrily if a policeman
insists that people refrain from moving the rope boundary further
into the street.

It should be no surprise, therefore, that campus youth engaged in some kind of mass activity will regard the police as agents
of repression. Thus, administration officials try to avoid bringing
uniformed police on the campus unless it seems matters are out of
hand and their presence needed. Such conditions usually do not
arise spontaneously but are built up over a period of time; the
pressures are almost visible. The administrator who looks ahead will
already have made contact with the police and, hopefully, have
obtained the assistance of nonuniformed police who may directly
observe the growing tension on campus and advise him when to call
for the uniformed police. These nonuniformed aides, as well as the
leaders of the police who may be called upon, should be trained in
crowd control and should be able to judge when to move in and
when to remain away. The individual policeman brought to a
campus should have some understanding about the attitudes and
conduct of college students. They should be trained to keep their
cool.

The procedure best designed to protect a campus near crisis
is to have a police contingent nearby, to be called upon when necessary but not to enter until internal efforts of control are shown likely
to fail.

The point to remember is that when a crowd fails to disperse
on a police order and the police are ordered to charge in order to
break up the assembly, there is very little discrimination that a
policeman can exercise when in the midst of the mob or even on its
edges. The charge is likely to hurt innocent people who have not
had the foresight to remove themselves from the scene. This is the
principal reason that the campus president asks trustees that he be
given discretion before he establishes conditions that make a police
charge, with accompanying mass arrests, the probable course of
action. A self-executing policy of the trustees that requires police to
be called immediately when possible trouble arises may well destroy
the order the trustees desire to maintain.

Considerable progress has been made in the last few years

in bringing police on campus for special training and in bringing them into various social science and psychology courses through which they can establish contact with students. The discussion of individual and social problems in this context is most constructive; they may be an important factor in establishing permanent peace on the campuses. Trustees should encourage instructional curricula for police on their campuses whenever feasible and within the scope of the institutional program.

A student writing in a campus newspaper under the headline "Pigs on Campus?" made this supporting statement (*Golden Gate Journal,* November 7, 1972):

> Most people, just from reading the title of this article, might easily have imagined the usual. You know what I mean, "STUDENT STRIKES, OCCUPATION OF CAMPUS BUILDINGS, DRAFT CARD BURNINGS," regular run of the mill campus activities. Well you've been duped, but not entirely. There are several dozen police officers on campus but they aren't in uniform. They are here to learn.
>
> Before you stop reading, dig this: I am not a police officer. I am not conservative. However, it may interest you to know that I am an Administration of Justice major, and that I am Black.
>
> Some of the individual police officers that I have met in some of my A.J. classes seem to be some very together cops. I've even run into a police chief who doesn't look, act, or talk too much like what I thought police chiefs did.
>
> My point is that many students are guilty of avoiding Ad.J. courses as electives because of their unadmitted fear of police.
>
> One of the real experiences of my life is being in a classroom atmosphere with "police types," where you can go and feel free to tell any police officers to take a leap. Well, folks, I enjoy this luxury whenever I'm ready.

A great deal was learned in the last decade about police on campus. Faculty members who were previously opposed to the presence of uniformed police under any circumstances began to realize that the community cannot depend upon extremists to cease and desist upon a gracious order or general appeal to reason. Reluctantly, but on the whole understandingly, faculty and students appear to have concluded that police are to be expected on campus in situations of violence as they are in any other part of the community. The mass of students who are attending our institutions of higher education want to continue their studies without interruption and also have become receptive to the idea that the campus cannot be a sanctuary for lawless action.

As always, preventive measures are the best answer to the problem. Student codes of conduct, developed and enforced with effective student participation, provide the best assurances for campus life that will not require the presence of police.

Trustee policy should require that uniformed police be called on campus to cope with injury or imminent danger of injury to persons or property. There should be cooperation with the police in order to control violence and prevent damage to persons and property. But the liaison with the police should be a carefully considered administrative matter, and the college president should be given some discretion in making and carrying out arrangements so that uniformed police are brought to the campus when needed and not prematurely.

When feasible, trustees should encourage administration and faculty to provide special training and courses for police designed to give them a better understanding of students and students a better appreciation of policemen and law enforcement.

Students and Faculty

With increased tuition, student pressure to have a say in the educational process will increase. ("What are we getting for our money?") Indeed, some student leaders demand that students be a third party in collective bargaining. It is doubtful whether the university could survive a three-party tug-of-war. But it must give a platform and participation to students.

In the future, faculty rather than the administration may be the principal target of student interest. Trustees may, from time to time, be cast in the role of arbiters.

12

STUDENT ACTIVITIES

One of the great changes in student life is the nature of student government. When the trustees were attending college, the chairman of the junior prom was an important campus personality. Today, if there is a junior prom, this office would be considered a household chore. The students say that the day of sandbox student government is over. They want to participate in the decisions affecting many important university policies: student codes of conduct and disciplinary proceedings; use of lobbyists to present student needs to the legislature; plans for new dormitories; tutorial help to disadvantaged students; public addresses by off-campus personalities. In short, the students want to play in the big league.

Student Government Aspirations

This desire to participate in the substantive matters of the university undoubtedly has been accelerated by the militancy of student activists. It has been further stimulated by the eighteen-year-old vote and the opportunities extended to influence national politics. (For some student leaders the college arena has become too small.) Still, the student activists continue to look down upon student government. They regard it, at best, as an agent of the establishment. Student government, they feel, must be a captive of the establishment because its financial resources, in one way or another, must be approved by the board of trustees and be subject to the financial controls required on student expenditures.

Some student official bodies are quite sophisticated. The presidents of the nineteen student bodies of the California State University and Colleges themselves have an association and a president and executive committee. They have a table alongside faculty and administration at trustee meetings. They are privileged to participate in matters of concern to students. They follow trustee agendas with care and do not hesitate to make proposals in the interests of the students. Usually they support policies that decentralize authority, that define and protect student rights (with a passing reference to responsibilities), and that ensure flexibility in academic requirements.

Obviously, a strong, responsible voice from students is most desirable. The difficulty is that student government seldom has the wholehearted support of student newspapers and is sniped at and attacked by the many independent campus groups. They have come out of the sandbox, but they are not yet firmly established in the major league.

On occasion an extremely activist group may be elected to control the student government. At one college such a group came into power determined to cut off practically all support for the athletic games program (including one or two breaches of game contracts) and concentrate the expenditure of student body money on salaries for tutors for disadvantaged high school students and other social projects. Administrative salaries zoomed, old-line college administrators who had managed student funds were fired, and pretty soon the student finances were in a mess. The attorney general of the state brought an action to impound the funds, and by the time the investigation was completed, much student power had been diffused.

Trustees should encourage the organization and administration of student government. If membership dues are mandatory, then the constitution of the student body should place reasonable limitations on the purposes for which funds can be expended. These purposes should not be subject to extreme change at the whim of a president or an executive committee. Every student's dollar is involved; it has been taken from him as part of the registration process. Usually considerable amounts of money are collected and spent, and there is no doubt that trustees should require a system of controls which will ensure accountability for their expenditure. In a way, student government is part of the educational process, and student officers, at the earliest stage of their participation in politics, should accept and respond to conditions of accountability. This means the employment of paid, experienced, and responsible auditors and controllers.

Trustees can encourage responsible student government in a number of ways. They can bring board officials into the discussion and resolution of problems affecting student affairs. The president of the student body might be one of the ex-officio board members. The board should approve policies that permit the college administration to delegate a certain area of responsibility to the student government subject to the requirement of financial accountability and controls. When students administer a large student union building, competitive athletics, and a substantial entertainment and social program, and perhaps also the book store, they are not engaging in sandbox activity. These are substantial business and financial programs and call for a great deal of judgment.

Trustees should encourage student government with authority over defined student affairs and accountable through employed professional fiscal agents.

Student Newspapers

The student newspaper has always been an interesting and exciting phenomenon. Every student editor usually feels that he has the power, authority, and ability of James Reston and uses the editorship to advance the only "right" position. Occasionally his enthusiasm and commitment carry him away, as when an editor of the *Daily Californian,* at the University of California at Berkeley, advised students to go down and seize People's Park for the people —an area of land belonging to the University which the Berkeley street people wanted for recreational purposes. But the trustees will remember that even during their own, quiet college days the student editor was usually a young man apart, a man with a mission, a slayer of administration dragons. I recall the editor who attacked a vice-president at the University of California for selling his house at an inflated price to the university; although ultimately the facts did not support the charge, the gentleman was effectively removed from his candidacy for the presidency of the university.

Allowances have always been made for student zeal and exuberance, but the lack of inhibition these days has taken forms that have worried trustees and administrators alike. In some cases, the four-letter word has become merely a useful expletive. Articles about sex and sexual habits, which in an earlier day would have resulted in instant expulsion, are printed and tolerated. Pictures far more explicit than *Playboy's* have decorated a number of campus publications.

Some trustees receive these publications and their hair grows white in a single night. It wasn't like that in their day. "These obscene and filthy publications must be stopped at once." But can they be? Are such publications actually obscene? A comparison with your local newspaper may answer this question. Or a walk through the night club part of your town. Ads in establishment newspapers for "adult" motion pictures set forth sexual details and allures which most student newspapers do not approach. The morals of our society have changed considerably, and the students live in this society. The trustees cannot expect that students will follow Cromwellian standards in Charles II's time.

It is established that the student press is part of the free press and cannot be subject to censorship. And rights and responsibilities are the same as those outside the campus. The question, then, is whether anything can or should be done to make the student press more "responsible"? The answer to both is probably yes, but the approaches vary. The procedure most desired by students and administration is to cut the relationship between the student newspaper and the institution. The newspaper becomes financially independent and is in full control of its news and editorial policies. Its nonassociation with the university is clearly shown on its masthead. Very successful student newspapers come within this category— self-financed student publications at Cornell, Dartmouth, Harvard, Michigan, and Yale. They depend upon subscriptions and advertising, not on institutional subsidy. Moreover, groups of students can publish smaller newspapers off campus independently and may be as propagandistic, spicy, and militant as the law allows. Independent student newspapers reflecting the particular interests of ethnic or other groups may be published and attract readers in the same way as they do in the general community.

A few years ago Norman Isaacs, president of the American Society of Newspaper Educators, headed a small commission that reviewed the campus press.[1] It concluded that when representative students were given full responsibility for their newspaper, the results usually demonstrated "sounder news coverage," "more thoughtful expression of viewpoints," and "closer attention to the expressed needs of student and faculty subscribers." They also attracted more volunteer staff members. It was found that the *Harvard Crimson* operated through an executive board of ten senior editors who had final authority, but the editorial policies were voted on by all news and editorial personnel; there was no faculty or administration advisor. The *Yale Daily News* was administered by a board of eight senior editors and also had no faculty or administration advisor. The *Darthmouth* has a board of proprietors of eight students, one alumnus, one faculty member, and one administration member which met three times a year, but editorial policies were determined solely by the editor. Independent campus newspapers are not required to carry institutional announcements and are treated by the administration pretty much like other media. Interviews with the president of the university are usually on-the-record.

If a newspaper staff and its institution agree that independence is desirable but find it impossible to dissolve the ties immediately, a three- or five-year program of liberation might be developed, with a gradual withdrawal of subsidy. There is no guarantee that the independent newspaper will make life more pleasant for the

[1] *Report of the Special Commission on the Campus Press,* University of California, December 1969.

authorities, but the authorities no longer need brood about their own responsibility.

Most campus newspapers, however, will not be able to procure sufficient resources to become financially independent. They will require some form of subsidy either from the institution or through an allocation of mandatory student fees.

If the campus newspaper is substantially supported by the institution so that the institution is its publisher, it is understandable that the administration will wish to be closer to the establishment of newspaper policies. It will feel that the taste shown by the student newspaper should be representative of an institution devoted to the better intellectual and cultural life.

A successful but sometimes unpopular procedure is to make the newspaper a laboratory project of the school's journalism department, actively operated by the students with faculty counsel but assisted by an advisory committee from the local commercial press. The students' objection to this type of arrangement is that it inhibits bold reporting and tends to be protective of the administration. On the other hand, the journalism department should offer some insulation to student writers, since the faculty should be particularly sensitive to the rights of a free press and expression. Student reporters and editors are still in the learning process and there is a certain logic that the publication of the campus newspapers should use the expertise of the faculty as a resource for guidance. The publications board should consist entirely or mostly of students, but the faculty should be represented, at least in an important advisory capacity. There is no other department of the institution that is so unusually able to combine theory and practice. If students are sufficently interested to enroll in the department and if the teaching is of value, it would seem to follow that they should be interested in putting the precepts to practice. The reporters need not be limited to students from the department. There are some excellent campus newspapers published under the guidance of the journalism department, and the fact that they use less four-letter words than some of the other newspapers should not be held against them. Examples: the *Columbus Missourian* (University of Missouri), *Daily Northwestern* (Northwestern University), the *Phoenix* (California State

University, San Francisco). The opposition of the commerical press to academic journalism departments as being too impractical seems to be waning as more reporters or ex-reporters join college staffs.

An in-between situation occurs when the newspaper is partly supported by student fees allocated by the student government. The student body then becomes the publisher and is quite resentful when its "own" press becomes critical about student officers and their programs. The student government may be entitled to some participation on the publishing board, but not immunity from criticism. The freedom of this student press might be better protected if the student body made a contract with respect to its subsidy and the newspaper would be distributed free to all students. Responsibility might be better assured if the faculty or newspaper fraternity contributed an expert advisor to a student publication board, with this board acting as actual publisher, assuming responsibility by holding regular meetings and giving a critique of the newspaper's performance.

Returning to the Isaacs commission report, it stressed two points for all general campus newspapers: First, the institution should not consider the newspaper to be its own trade paper, required to give first consideration to its announcements and programmed news. If the newspaper cannot provide sufficient space for institutional announcements, the institution should from time to time circulate an independent newsletter. Second, the student editors should operate their newspaper according to the canons governing the publication of the best newspapers in the country, demanding fair and accurate reporting, providing space for opinions counter to editorial policy, and, in short, being responsible.

It should be board policy to encourage the model (entirely independent, sponsored by the student government, or sponsored by the university) appropriate to the institution, after receipt of a study and recommendation from the president.

Student newspapers are part of the free press. The preferred arrangement is that the student newspaper operate independently of the institution, with its own financing and its own student publications board. If institutional financial support and sponsorship is necessary, then one effective arrangement is to have the newspaper

*operate with the guidance of the institution's journalism depart-
ment, under a student board and with a senior journalism professor
advisor.*

Campus Speakers

Practically every campus has its Hyde Park area, where any
speaker may sound off on "the issues." This is free and protected
speech, but "filthy speech" (obscentity for its own sake) is subject
to discipline. Use of university property may also be regulated to
disallow programming or arranging for unlawful acts outside the
campus; for example, a rally to instruct students on the seizure and
occupation of the city hall.

The time, place, and manner of assemblies may be subject
to reasonable regulation. Any recognized student group may request auditorium or free-speech area space for an event, giving the
hour, speaker, and expected attendance. The aspects that bother
trustees are the frequency with which militant leftist speakers obtain
the platform compared with moderate or conservative speakers and
the fees charged by certain of these speakers, which are paid from
student body sources. Most boards would be happy if the administration could screen all speakers and permit only those who are "acceptable." Since this procedure is neither feasible nor desirable,
most boards would wish to provide for a balanced program—the
radical followed (not necessarily the same day) by a conservative—
so that the students could evaluate the opposing viewpoints.

From an educational standpoint, this attitude is unassail-
able. The students should have the opportunity to hear the pros and
cons. But it is the sensationalist of the moment, the controversial
speaker, who attracts the audience; a sound speaker taking the overall view may have little drawing power. (A symphony can be given
equal time with a rock concert, but the audiences will differ in
make-up and probably in number.) Thus, interested student groups
will bring pressure to hear an Angela Davis, William Kunstler,
Huey Newton, Allen Ginsberg, Benjamin Spock, and occasionally
a William Buckley, and to pay him a fee up to two thousand dollars.
These are speakers who, in most instances, can be counted upon to
pour it on the establishment, and students have been receptive.

A condition that a question period must be available, that a panel of "objective" faculty be permitted to examine the speaker or to comment, may be effective. But this is not a classroom or academic situation. The money is paid and the students expect the star to perform without being accompanied by home talent.

The board might authorize a president to put some reasonable limit on the total amount to be expended on outside speakers as a student government budgetary item, if the board has authority to approve such budgets. (If student government on its own fixed total and specific limits, it would be more significant.) It can require a report on fees paid beyond a fixed amount and a list of speakers who appear on the campus. Rarely can it provide that the president may refuse a request for an outside speaker even when the condition of his presence may be likely to cause possible violence. The law seeks to protect the speaker from the crowd, rather than the reverse. However, if the speaker requires conditions totally at variance with a university environment, refusal is possible. Huey Newton was invited to speak on a campus but required that he be accompanied by his armed guards on stage at all times in order to insure his personal safety. The college president refused to consent to this condition on the ground that such a platform arrangement was not appropriate to an academic environment.

In developing a policy on outside campus speakers the trustees should consider the following points: First, they should give credit to the maturity of most students, who will lose interest in paying high fees for big names who deliver dull speeches or for other persons who are purely propagandists. Second, they should bear in mind that during their college years students are exposed to a great variety of ideas—in classrooms, in assemblies, over television, on and off the campus. The message of the outside speaker, therefore, is small compared with all of the other influences. Third, they should remember that one purpose of the university is to serve as critic of society and that the scales on controversial issues will not always be even. Fourth, they should realize that the greatest defense against extremism, paid for or free, rests in the institution itself. If the teaching insists on critical evaluation as a habit of mind, if the university inculcates a healthy skepticism, the outside speaker will have to prove his worth to make any mark. Finally, for certain situations involving important immediate issues, where an influential outside speaker may be guilty of grave distortions of facts, the trustees should insist there be a procedure agreed upon by students, faculty, and administration through which an effective reply can be given—whether by another speaker or through the campus newspaper, closed-circuit television, or other media—so that the students are fairly informed.

The most difficult job of the trustees, on occasion, is to convince faculty and students that they cannot test public tolerance to its outer limits and expect public and legislative support. In other words, avant-garde conduct may be technically lawful but highly prejudicial to the institution's ongoing operations. Elsewhere in this book some situations are described which have tested these limits. There are events that embody questions of principle, and that, though popularly distasteful, do call for the trustees to defend the institution against all who attack. But at other times, unwise decisions are made within the institution which the trustees may be required to explain, adjust, or remedy, but which, in good conscience, they cannot defend as conduct becoming to higher education. They have the further obligation to set forth their own and the public attitude to the institution in an attempt to prevent needless spectacular incidents of no significant academic consequence but injurious to the essential program of the institution because of their probable effect on public support.

Trustee policy on campus speakers should recognize that such speakers constitute a small part of the educational influences on students; the time, place, and manner of speeches may be regulated; "balance" of speeches can be urged but not ordered.

13

OBTAINING FUNDS FOR PUBLIC INSTITUTIONS

An important function of boards of trustees of public institutions has to do with requesting funds from the finance department, the governor, and the legislature. Too often the trustees adopt the budget request prepared by the institution's administration and passively await the results. They should not hesitate to tell their story more directly—to the appropriate executive agencies and legislature and to the public. Usually this calls for action by the board chairman and a small, informed committee of trustees. Of course, unless the committee is informed and can demonstrate its knowledge of budget details and its conviction as to their necessity, it is better to

177

forego this effort. But the presence of influential trustees on the
legislative battle line can be of immense benefit to the institution.

Presenting Budgets Affirmatively

The condition of success is credibility. The trustees must
have a record of fiscal responsibility in operations. They also should
have a reputation for making supportable budgetary requests, for
asking for what is needed, taking into consideration a realistic approach to the state (or local) finances. Circumstances may compel
them to point out alternatives, to state that if the budget is cut by
so much, this program may have to be terminated or that number
of admissions curtailed. Almost every institution, at one time or another, has had to adjust to hard times, but the board should make
clear that any diminution of service will be resolved in the interest
of maintaining quality.

This posture—affirmative to obtain appropriations to meet
demonstrated needs, yet restained to show credibility—is difficult to
establish and maintain. State or local fiscal authorities may believe
that the board is overselling, faculty that the board is underselling.
I have heard faculty members contend that it is better for trustees,
administration, and faculty to go down the fiscal drain, in one boat,
united, with colors flying than to have the board compromise or
accept the possible. Certainly if the institution is about to receive a
mortal blow, heroics are called for; but they will never produce results if they become an annual ritual.

The trustees' biggest selling job may be to the institution
itself—in terms of explaining competing public needs, priorities, disagreeable alternatives, and the need to maintain public good will.
So long as the trustees can preserve or bring to the institution flexibility in expenditure, so that maximum transfers may be made
within a more limited budget, the academy may prove to be understanding and cooperative, though still unhappy.

In interpreting the trustees' obligations to approve and
secure a proper budget, the board should relate to the state or local
fiscal situation but not be intimidated by it. The Board should not
assume the duty of raising revenues or programming changes in the

tax structure in order to obtain its appropriations; it should determine the institution's true needs, including essential innovation, and fight for the reasonable and possible.

The struggle for the budget in its initial stages may be with the state fiscal and auditing authorities. The finance bureau auditor prefers to work with mathematical formulas of class contact hours, library books per student, fixed faculty-student and student-space ratios, and to compute the results to yield the perfect budget. He may be upset when he notes a low number of average contact hours, say from six to seven. His eyes may boggle when he finds a number of administrative salaries higher than those of any of the highest paid state officials. He may see waste in the purchase or retention of valuable books rarely used. In one review, for instance, an auditor recommended that the University of California sell some of its rare-book collections because of their limited use and apply the proceeds for general educational puproses. He regarded the collections as surplus jewels not necessary to a dowager who needs hard dollars to meet her grocery bills.

Some fiscal representatives require continuing education. Average class contact hours may stay put or actually decrease as tutorial, counseling, and other independent services are increased. The value of research in a great university cannot be measured by its applied results alone, considerable as they may be. Salaries will be high for administrators directly responsible for spending scores of millions of dollars; so will those for medical and law professors, whose services are sought professionally outside of the university. Finally, the university must not be penalized because, through accident or design, its library has become the custodian of a noble portion of the elusive past.

Here is a place for the trustee to act, and an establishment trustee can be especially effective. When the business executive speaks for fiscal flexibility, for a total, not narrow, view of faculty work, for the payment of competitive compensation in the field of higher education, he is heeded and his influence is felt. Words like these of Regent Edward Carter, in defense of the university budget, delivered at a regents' meeting of the University of California and widely reported, are worth repeating:

The president of the university is underpaid for the kind of position he holds . . . I think that job is worth at least 50 percent more [than $53,500]. The governor and the Department of Finance are not the best judge of what balance there should be between instruction and research . . . In your pursuit of economics it is extremely important to realize that you are dealing with a very fragile instrument. No doubt some economies can be effected without affecting the university's quality, and I would strongly support these. On the other hand, in recent years, the state has gotten a nationwide reputation of having an "anti-university" attitude and of not being the best place [for faculty] to come to. We won't know for fifteen or twenty years whether we have suffered by not attracting the topmost doctoral students and faculty around the country.

Trustees of state institutions must maintain active relationships with officials in the executive and legislative branches, and those of community colleges with officials in local and state agencies. Many of these contacts are required by law, particularly in fiscal matters; others will simply keep officials informed of the programs, problems, and governance of the institution so that when matters come before these officials, they will give them fair consideration.

For the most part this building up of confidence is a function of the college administration. The trustees enter the picture only occasionally—perhaps at academic or social functions attended by legislative or other officials or possibly at other events that have nothing to do with the institution. The best relationship a trustee can have with a legislator or other official is a one-to-one relationship of trust, so that when a problem arises either may call the other and be confident that what he hears about the institution is an honest statement. Ultimately, replies to official questions must go through their proper channels, but a knowledgeable trustee can do a vast amount of good by helping an inquiring public official to obtain a prompt reply.

Trustees should be affirmative in presenting budgets to meet demonstrated needs, yet restrained to show credibility. Once these needs are determined, the board should fight for them. Trustees should maintain continuing liaison with legislative and public officials.

Private Funds for Public Institutions

Unlike trustees of private institutions, those of public institutions are not expected to raise funds to support the basic educational program. The concept of public institutions is that they should be tax supported. Nevertheless, there are areas that public money does not touch: special library acquisitions, programs for visual arts and music, and various kinds of valuable scientific, anthropological, and sociological research. Moreover, there are seldom sufficient scholarships. Trustees can be effective in encouraging and procuring the contribution of tax-free gifts for these purposes. The private endowments given to public institutions may be the margin that makes greatness possible.

In considering how to raise private funds from sources other than foundations, trustees must consider three matters.

First is the question of legitimacy. Is it acceptable for tax-supported institutions to seek private support? True, many public universities have received substantial gifts and endowments in the past, but at a time when higher education funds are in short supply, is a campaign for funds to augment the resources of a public institution fair to the private universities and colleges which are increasingly desperate about balancing their budgets? Usually a public institution cannot divert loyalties from private institutions, but it can appeal to similar sentiments and loyalties of their alumni or to citizens in the area it serves. These are not people who would be strongly motivated to give property or money to private universities and colleges. The appeals to individuals are, as between the public and private sectors, essentially noncompetitive.

The solicitation of corporations, however, may be competitive. Public institutions have justified their efforts with corporations on the ground that the distinction between public and private institutions is becoming more blurred—federal and state contracts, scholarship, and other funds are being distributed to the private institutions, and public institutions have a long history of receiving private funds. Furthermore, many public institutions may provide curricula of direct interest to industries or unions (for instance, a community college may offer a restaurant and hotel training program) which may wish to assist with special grants for equipment and scholarships. It is quite arguable that private institutions should not have exclusive rights to solicit private corporations.

A second and greater problem is the danger of legislative offset. If there is no clear legislative policy supporting the principle of special private funding for public institutions, the legislature will tend to count the income, if not the principal, of private funding as a resource to be deducted in arriving at net appropriations. The solicitation efforts then become self-defeating. One way to minimize this negative effect is to procure funds to finance specific projects or capital outlays (of the kind previously described) since the legislature must recognize the restrictions.

Third, the multiversity has its own peculiar problems. It may wish to raise funds and allocate them to its various campuses and to enlist community leaders at or near each campus to participate in the general fund raising. This procedure may prove difficult. Individual givers wish to relate to a name campus, to the physical facilities in a specific location, to local tradition and needs. They are not attracted to subsidizing the centralized headquarters, an abstraction of many campuses. Therefore, the central agency should encourage the procurement by local leaders of local money to be expended on local campuses.

However, projects involving innovation on a number of campuses or research projects for the common good of all campuses, are best obtained by the central office in the name of or through the multiversity trustees. Also, there are certain projects involving individual donors which may be best initiated by the central agency— for instance, an art exhibit for the use of all campuses or visiting lectureships from abroad for the benefit of several campuses. The allocation between local and central agencies should be carefully worked out, otherwise fund raisers will be tripping each other on the same unyielding doorsteps.

Fund raising for public institutions, then, should be in areas of needs unmet and unlikely to be met by legislative appropriation. It should be understood by budgetary bodies, the legislature, and the public that such funds do not duplicate regular operational requirements and should not be deducted from appropriations. The gifts should result in plus, not minus, moneys.

Trustees of public institutions should support private fund raising to meet needs not met by appropriated tax money and for which the institution will not be penalized by reduced appropriations. Gifts for special projects afford the most protection.

Tuition

I have already indicated that trustees, as a point of educational policy, should strive to keep tuition to a minimum. However, tuition has its strictly financial aspects, and some student funding, either directly or through subsidy, is usually necessary in order to balance the budgets of senior institutions.

The basic question is which agency should have final approval of tuition fees.

Under the state constitution or legislative delegation the trustees of each public institution or segment of institutions or a consolidated board may be authorized to charge tuition (Arkansas, University of California, Illinois, North Carolina, New York, Michigan, Missouri, Oregon, South Carolina, Tennessee, Virginia, Wisconsin).

A super or coordinating board, by constitution or statute may be delegated the right to fix tuition (Ohio, New Jersey, Kentucky, Oklahoma).

The legislature itself may fix tuition (Massachusetts, New Mexico, Texas).

Regardless of who has the authority to make a final determination, other government agencies may exercise considerable influence. In Illinois the coordinating council makes substantial recommendations, although the institution determines; in Massachusetts the institutions recommend, although the legislature decides; and in other states the governor and legislature may bring considerable pressure, although the institutional board has the legal authority. The various segments will, of course, bring pressure on a super or coordinating board, which makes the tuition decisions.

As a practical matter, the legislature will always be in a position to bring heavy pressure. Indeed, it can be argued that the legislature should always fix tuition, for then the legislators will be clearly responsible for the actions taken. They may be less inclined to fix a high tuition at the same time that they hold down on appropriations. However, if the trustees already have the authority to determine the tuition schedule, they should try to retain it, because it means greater flexibility in operations.

If the legislature makes its appropriations for higher education in the fall or early spring for the next academic year, the trustees are then able to decide what additional amounts from students are needed to operate the institution or to what extent economies may reduce possible tuition charges. But should the legislative practice be to appropriate late in the spring for the coming academic year, then the trustees, by setting the fees in advance, are in a better bargaining position with the legislature on the tuition issue (at least for the succeeding year), for the legislature will then have to appropriate in relation to the fee schedule or else be held responsible for compelling the trustees to change the schedule.

The manner in which tuition is charged can well affect the quality of undergraduate and graduate programs. Trustees may determine to average tuition costs and probably charge larger sums (in relation to costs) in the undergraduate than in the graduate area in order to conserve some of the university's important functions in the upper division and graduate programs.[1]

If a super or coordinating board has the power to make allocations of a master appropriation to its various campuses, then it may be logical for it to bear the responsibility for establishing tuition rates. Yet it still seems preferable that the operating institution continue to have the authority to determine tuition charges in order to maintain flexibility in operations.

Although the legislature plays a decisive role in determining tuition increases, the specific adjustments in rates should be fixed by the operating board.

Economizing

When public funds are materially reduced for public universities and colleges, trustees may make adjustments in various

---

[1] But lower fees for the lower division may increase opportunity.

ways, following the recommendations of the president in consultation with the faculty. The actions should be in the form of policy determinations to be implemented by administration and faculty. Programs and course commitments to students currently studying for degrees must be honored or requirements duly adjusted so that the students can still finish when they anticipated. The following itemization is not intended to be exhaustive or to suggest any diminution of effort to procure alternative sources of income and avoid unnecessary deletions.

When retrenchment is necessary, the institution may begin by terminating programs for which grants are no longer available, such as federal grants for specific research contracts. It may also cut back professional or semiprofessional schools for which reliable data demonstrate there will be a probable lack of academic or economic demand for a long period of time. Exotic cultural courses attended by only a few students and other courses or departments for which there is small demand may be reduced or eliminated—for example, those in dead languages or in historic forms of live languages. Language requirements may be lowered when they are not essential to the major or as a component of general studies. Certain courses may be allowed to disappear as professors retire.

Other ways of economizing are to defer or stretch out the building of new capital facilities (but balance this against the increased construction costs involved); to adhere to the organizational table regarding the award of tenure; to employ more replacement teaching personnel at lower ranks or on a part-time basis; to increase tuition within reasonable limits; to charge a student extra for courses he takes that substantially exceed the number needed for a degree.

The institution should be particularly careful about initiating any graduate programs or costly innovative programs (but initial costs may be necessary in order to effect ultimate savings). For other belt tightening, it may increase teaching unit or instructional contact loads or class size where appropriate (faculty opposition may be expected); increase plant use in the evenings and weekends to meet student demand (it will also provide maximum cost-benefit statistics); require controls to prevent abuse of administrative services (limiting duplicating and stenographic services, telephone calls to outside areas; and motor pool services); and control essentially unproductive travel allowances. This brings up the question of the value of some (not all) professional meetings; faculty contend that many of these meetings are necessary to maintain quality instruction, to keep abreast of their fields, and to recruit personnel at the professional "slave markets."

In effecting economies, the trustee should pay attention to the conservation of unique offerings. If through historical or other accident, yours is the only institution that gives a particular course of study or maintains a long-established line of inquiry, it may be part of your trust to do everything possible to preserve it; to terminate it may mean some savings of current income but a great loss of cultural capital. In the interests of conserving such an area of study, the faculty may be willing to make some adjustments in their teaching load; perhaps an involuntary increase may be justified.

In the search for economy, trustees may be requested to engage outside, neutral management-research institutes to study their institution and recommend maximum use of plant, operational changes, and economies. Often these outside studies function like a computer; the administration controls the inputs and the outputs are pretty well as expected but at considerable expense. Self-evaluation, together with fiscal reviews by other state agencies (such as a coordinating council, department of finance, or legislative analyst), usually produce more constructive recommendations than do private contract surveys.

What must be guarded against in retrenchment efforts is overeconomizing that actually results in overexpenditure in terms of educational effectiveness. It is possible by removing clerical help and teaching assistants from professors to save substantial administrative expense, but the result may be fewer demands on the students for examinations or term papers or less teaching and more clerical work by the more highly paid professors. Query, what has been saved? It may be possible, through the extensive part-time employment of marginal teachers, to keep the classrooms filled from morning until night, providing mediocre instruction for masses of impassive students; the statistics may be phenomenal; but the education may be deplorable. Moreover, it may be possible to limit access to the point of reducing student enrollment or materially to cut down offerings and reduce instructional personnel. Indeed, it may be possible to operate a billion-dollar plant so economically that education may be eliminated from the campus almost entirely. There is no waste quite so destructive as economy which amounts to an abandonment of purpose.

Economies may be essential, but evaluate them before adoption. Some economies are simply too expensive to implement.

14

RELATIONSHIPS WITH THE FEDERAL GOVERNMENT

The most significant new relationships established by higher education in recent years are those with the United States Government. The Federal Government has had an interest in higher education for over one hundred years. Through the Morrill Act of 1862, which provided for granting of public lands for the establishment of educational institutions, the land-grant college system was founded. Under this act many states established their institutions, first to promote only mechanics and agriculture, but subsequently broadened to the entire curriculum of a liberal arts college or university. But apart from creating one or two units of ROTC on campus, the state institution had minimal relationships with the Federal Government.

Recent Background

When Sputnik went up in 1957 it began a fundamental change. Jarred by the belief that the United States had fallen behind Soviet Russia because American higher education was deficient in the sciences and stressed a soft liberal arts curriculum, Congress passed the National Defense Education Act, which provided universities and colleges with special financial assistance for strengthening their curriculum in science, mathematics, and language. It is strange that one of the most important legislative enactments bearing on the quality of higher education should have been embedded in a defense policy; but it was, and it stimulated the space program and associated industries to speedy and amazing achievements.

The trouble was that the program became too specialized, too narrow in its purposes and training, and too expensive. Suddenly it was greatly curtailed, and too many young physicists found themselves unemployed or compelled to take menial jobs in supermarkets and elsewhere in order to provide their families with subsistence. Certainly one lesson to be learned from this experience is that when the federal government develops a massive program that will heavily affect the career orientation of young people, it should have the further duty to provide for continuing education to redirect such personnel to other professional work of equal status or worth when it pulls back on its original program. And, second, the experience shows that it is not fair to students to train them in such a narrow area of scientific work that they will find it almost impossible to adjust when the specific program that created their first opportunities is greatly curtailed or withdrawn. If many boards of trustees had acted in concert, they might have pressured the executive branch and Congress to provide enough money to redirect this talent into other engineering and scientific areas subsidized by federal grants as necessary, easing the transition for these highly paid specialists and avoiding much frustration, bitterness, personal economic disaster, and social waste.

In the last ten years, the Federal Government has entered a number of fields important to higher education. It has provided capital grants enabling institutions to build new facilities; it has financed a substantial scholarship program through grants and loans, particularly to assist the disadvantaged; and it has given grants to stimulate academic innovation. This last category has caused institutions to revise curriculum and create new programs and reorganize old programs, sometimes to give them a new look and new label in order to qualify for federal assistance. It is probably too early to judge whether federally financed innovations have brought forth any major educational breakthroughs, but they are making important changes possible.

Alongside these programs has run a federal contract or project system for financing research. These grants have been especially effective in the sciences and unquestionably have affected the direction of university research and have contributed materially to much needed general overhead. Critics say these grants have caused too much academic empire building and diverted the energies of too many good teachers. But, admittedly, they have financed a tremendous amount of worthwhile research in many fields, including (though to a much lesser degree) the humanities. Not nearly enough has been accomplished in improving teaching methods, but that is another story.

The Higher Education Amendments of 1972 appeared to provide for even more aid to higher education. The act extended aid into two important areas: first, the government may provide students with direct grants (called BEOG—Basic Education Opportunity Grants) so that the students can choose the insitution they wish to enroll in; second, for the first time the government may give general operating grants to institutions in financial need. This latter category has not been funded. Congress appropriated somewhat less than 25 percent of $622 million for BEOG grants for fiscal 1973 and a modest percentage for the same type of grants for fiscal 1974, reserving the bulk of student aid to be administered by institutions, as in the past—through college work-study, National Defense Student loans, and Supplementary Educational Opportunity Grants. The Congress still prefers that institutions administer aid rather than that students determine the institutions to be aided. HEW requested that federal aid be directed to low income students; the Congress still wanted institutions to assist a substantial number of students from the middle income group.

Higher education aid has been reorganized under an assistant secretary of education into three categories: the Office of Education administering the student subsidies; the National Institute of Education providing financing for research projects; and the Fund for Advancement of Post Secondary Education for innovation, with a $10 million allocation for 1973 and $15 million for 1974 and an administrative promise of much larger amounts if the program produces results.

Thus, the federal government imprint has been felt almost everywhere in higher education. For a long time this assistance was thought to be benign and not to interfere with the ongoing operations of the university. But in less than fifteen years, the combination of research contracts, innovation projects, scholarship assistance, and capital advances has made higher education realize that it has become a partial dependent of the federal government. Recently reductions in federal appropriations have profoundly affected research and curriculum offerings. Student aid is comparatively the most important category of assistance. The more aid that is channeled through direct student grants, the more private institutions expect to benefit. Public institutions probably prefer that most student aid continue to be administered on an institutional basis.

There has been much wringing of hands over reduced federal assistance. Educators have complained that insufficient federal scholarship and research funds are being made available to meet the demand and that institutions will not be able to procure much needed supplementary aid for operating or capital needs from other government sources such as revenue-sharing funds granted to states and localities. The federal government certainly should make some institutional grants to help meet higher education needs in poor states, the costs of educational or research programs stimulated by federal career demands, and the expense of instructing nonresident students from other states. The proper scope of all federal aid is a subject for legitimate controversy, but, it should be noted, limits on the kinds of federal aid limit the possibilities of federal control. Perhaps academic institutions cannot have it both ways. If they desire more independence from the federal government, they may have to make do with less direct federal help or at least with fewer categories of federal assistance. And it should be further observed that the problem of federal aid is not only uncertainty of amount but also uncertainty of policy. What is required is a long-term and stable program of federal aid upon which higher education can depend for a part of its resources.

Trustees should seek from the federal government reasonably stable and long term policies of financial aid in order to assure educational opportunity to students and to ease the financial burden of their institution. They should demand that any new large-scale graduate-training programs include both long- and short-term plans for the use of such manpower.

Nondiscrimination and Affirmative Action

Against this background of federal involvement let us consider the serious controversies that have arisen between the academic community and the HEW over hiring and related federal policies. Under Executive Order 11,246, HEW seeks to enforce two concepts of employment in higher education: nondiscrimination and affirmative action. Nondiscrimination means that the employment policies of an institution will not—in statement or implementation—deny equal employment opportunity to any person on the grounds of race, color, religion, sex, or national origin. Affirmative action means an institution must make efforts to recruit and hire women and minorities so as not to passively perpetuate the inequities of past discrimination.

HEW contends that it is not requiring an institution to establish quotas for women and minority employment, or to employ specific numbers of such persons in each department or school by such and such a date. It is only demanding that the institution state its "goals"—or targets—for such employment, against which progress can be measured. If the institution fails to reach its projected goals, this does not automatically mean that the institution is in default, but that the reasons for failure should be examined and explained. If a satisfactory explanation cannot be given, the institution is in danger of losing its federal assistance programs because of noncompliance—a heavy sanction, and HEW knows it.

Higher education is most suspicious of the terms "quotas" and "goals" as being, in practice, almost interchangeable. In numerical terms, a goal is a quota; if you do not reach it, you are on the defensive. If, to be cautious in your commitment, you set a goal that is regarded as too low, it appears from the start that you are not sincere in providing equality of opportunity. But if, to show a high commitment to social policy, you set too high a goal, you may very well wind up a defendant.

The academic group is also gravely concerned about what happens if a marginal or nonqualified teacher is employed and then is not reappointed or promoted. What if in certain fields, such as ethnic studies, the minority person claims that the usual academic qualifications do not apply to his type of work and that therefore it would be discriminatory to use them? Each case is a potential problem of discrimination, with the burden of proof on the institution. The Equal Employment Opportunities Commission or its successor, the Office of Civil Rights, investigates and enforces claims of individuals of discrimination, and may use the affirmative action commitments of HEW and failures to achieve as evidence of violation of the federal civil rights acts.

This situation requires some further clarification. The Federal Government is certainly right about initiating a policy of equal treatment and affirmative action to achieve it, but it is wrong, I believe, in the timetables it has in mind. It is a disservice to minorities and students to place nonqualified persons on the academic ladder and then freeze them into tenure in a situation that can affect the future of higher education for close to forty years. It is a disservice to encourage promises to academic employees, which, if educational quality is to be preserved, will be broken. Moreover, if persons who should not be employed are later removed at a greater rate than their colleagues, it will appear that discriminatory action has taken place and the institution will probably find itself in a tangled forest of litigation. It does not protect any of the parties for the federal agency to say it is only concerned with what is reasonable if it sets in motion premises and procedures that are unreasonable. With ambiguous phrases, the situation is bound to get out of hand.

In addition, this is a very difficult time for higher education to make quick changes in its academic employment profile. The increase in academic employment is static or slow because student enrollments are static or decreasing. It is a time following a period of great expansion when a tremendous number of young instructors and professors have been added to meet the expansion requirements of the sixties. Thus, the turnover in the next ten to twenty years will not be nearly as substanial as in recent years. The only way to realize HEW employment goals would be to fire many present faculty members and substitute others.

The tragedy is that the situation is partly manufactured. Institutions all over the country have been exerting great effort to obtain faculty members from minority ethnic groups, but they are not yet available in the numbers desired. They can and will be made available in the coming years after equality in the educational process has been given the chance it requires. But what a mistake it would be for the Federal Government to establish a policy that would result in weak representatives of minorities being frozen into academic positions, so that in later years the strong members of the minorities will be barred from the opportunity.

HEW spokesmen have frequently said they do not ask the institution to hire nonqualified persons. "Standards of performance and qualifications that are not themselves discriminatory," they say, "need not be abandoned or compromised in order to hire unqualified women and minorities." But if this premise is truly meant, then it should be agreed that the targets should be realistic.

The situation with women is somewhat different than that with minorities. Women not only constitute a majority of the population; their academic performance has also always been competitive. Given their opportunity, women would be able to absorb many of the vacancies. If they are the better applicants, they should be employed.

At the bottom of this trouble is the proposal that somehow we must depart from the principle of individual merit in order to right the agonizing social wrongs of the past. Of all of our social institutions, higher education has placed the greatest emphasis on individual merit. Sometimes it has not been true to itself on standards, but by and large it seeks higher performance; it has felt an obligation to be the model of performance. Its calling is to inspire and to guide. It should not be compelled to forfeit its role by prematurely attempting to reach unfair and improper employment goals—unfair to white applicants when they are clearly superior; unfair to the superior minority applicants of the future; and unfair to the students who will be instructed by the faculties of the present and future. By all means require the institution to make a thorough canvas of minority and women candidates when there are vacancies, give them the benefit of the doubt in a case of apparent equality of qualifications and hold a vacancy for a reasonable time; but do not set up an employment schedule dependent on reduced standards of performance.

Finally, the question that sooner or later must be considered by Americans inside and outside of higher education: should all professions and vocations be represented by persons from ethnic groups in their proportion to the population? This is a quota or goal system carried to its final absurdity. It is only a question of time when underrepresented minorities from other groups—Italians, Poles, Czechs, and so on—will ask for their appropriate representation. Only the most sophisticated computer-programming will be able to take the jumble of women, whites, blacks, Indians, Chinese, Japanese, Filipinos, Samoans, Spanish-surnamed, and so on, and come out with the answers that will provide for properly constituted university faculties, industries, agriculture, the Green Bay Packers, and the Harlem Globetrotters.

What I am suggesting here is that the principle that each person may be judged on individual merit is still the noblest personnel principle of all. It cuts across divisive ethnic lines; it is intended to fulfill the guarantee of the individual right to pursue life, liberty, and happiness. Of course, to effectuate this guarantee, there must be equality of opportunity and this calls for massive educational, economic, and political effort to lay the foundation for equal treatment. Let us remember that the ideal is to enable every person to reach his own potential and compete in his chosen field or fields with every other person, not simply to be placed as a representative of a constituency.

There is some evidence that the Federal Government wishes the regional accrediting agencies, which determine the academic status of institutions of higher education, to become the enforcement instruments of affirmative-action employment policies and in other ways to police the compliance with federal requirements. The accrediting agencies are shying away from the responsibility, stating that their expertise is in curriculum and program and not in these other areas. This is an issue worth careful consideration. If the accrediting agencies do not take on certain of these obligations, the Federal Government may establish accrediting procedures of its own. Possibly, the accrediting agencies can become educational brokers to help produce realistic federal policies by fairly reporting on the efforts and problems of the institutions they deal with.

Trustees must wrestle with this prime problem of relationships to the Federal Government. Most institutions must accept federal assistance in order to compete and survive. Trustees should approve employment policies that are necessary to comply with law and that at the same time support the quality of the institution. Trustees familiar with employment in industry should encourage every effort to achieve fair employment practices and should defend the institution against unfair demands. Meanwhile, the establishment of a generous nontenured-to-tenured ratio will help keep opportunities open to a substantial degree.

Trustees must implement attainable affirmative action policies. But they should oppose if necessary any ill considered short term employment requirements in higher education which would damage equal opportunities for minorities (including much talent in the process of being trained) and adversely affect the quality of education.

15

RELATIONSHIPS WITH THE PUBLIC

In facing the public the trustees should consistently emphasize the achievements and contributions of the institution. They should point out that every institution is a community in itself, fairly certain to have its percentage of troubles and errors, like any human enterprise. They should not, of course, defend wrongdoing or error in themselves but ask the public to judge their institution on the totality of their program, not on some deleterious act or some isolated instance of poor judgment. If, however, the cases are not isolated, if the educational process or quality is suffering from weak administration, then the board must take firm steps to correct the situation, take the necessary actions in policy and personnel, make their actions known, and go on to other business.

In the following sections, I will discuss the college in relation to alumni, media, parents, and the public as a whole.

Alumni

The Board of Overseers of Harvard University is elected by alumni. It is responsible for all of the important constitutional acts of the Harvard corporation and the several faculties, and it has the duty to inspect every part of the university and make recommendations to the administrative authority. Together with the president and treasurer it consents to the election of the seven persons who constitute the executive control of finance and education of the corporation.

This extent of alumni participation at the highest level of governance may not work for most public institutions, but many require some alumni board members, and this condition in several instances is set by statute. The fact that the prestigious private institutions recognize the important contributions alumni can make to the life and progress of the institution is indicative of their value.

Whether the institution is public or private, the members of the community most familiar and sympathetic with it are the alumni. They alone have the ties of experience and tradition which make their association unique. They know their college, most are appreciative of their academic experience, and a great many, in one way or another, wish to contribute to its support.

Of course, the institution the alumni knew was the one that they attended. The passing years may have changed their alma mater, yet they may think of its projects and problems in old terms. Some think that alumni participation and influence come out of the past and are necessarily restrictive, but this is sheer conjecture and does not reflect the situation. In the first place, alumni graduated at different times and represent a variety of experiences, not a single past. Second, notwithstanding new campus life styles and the generation gap, alumni have continued to support the private institutions with millions of dollars and the public institutions with great effort in the political arena. Alumni interests vary, of course. There are certain alumni whose idea of their university is totally embodied in its athletic teams. They will recruit, provide scholarships, support coaches, and do everything possible to produce a winning team. So long as the institution itself is similarly committed, these alumni can ride through life as though they had never graduated.

To make this comment is not to deny the pleasant spirit and camaraderie that are embraced in this form of alumni activity. But most alumni are more serious about their institution. They are genuinely concerned about campus problems, student restlessness, having a quality faculty, avoiding deficits, and the gamut of educational issues. What is needed in order to reap the full benefit of this concern is a flow of information to the alumni and occasional reunions on campus so that they may see for themselves what is going on.

Many alumni publications are of a high order in this respect. Some tend to be preoccupied with athletic news and class gossip, but the effective periodicals are those which include reports from the president or the chancellor, which discuss the achievements and discoveries of the faculty, which illustrate successful teaching techniques and methods, and which give the alumni reader a sense of being with the current show. The publications should be frank about unsolved problems and indicate how the administration plans to deal with them—coeducational dormitories, minority pressures, dropouts, drugs. With an informed and interested alumni the public university will have its defenders in the legislature and the executive mansion.

The on-campus reunions are also important. Usually they occur at important anniversaries such as the tenth or twenty-fifth. There may be many other visits in between, but on the important anniversaries special programs are usually arranged. There should always be an opportunity for the alumni to meet with distinguished professors and to participate in the excitement of the academic atmosphere. Certainly on the more important occasions several trustees should put in their appearance so that the alumni are made aware of the governing board and of the kind of lay leadership the institution provides. If the public relations of a university or college with its alumni are not successful, the probability is that the relations with the general public will not be very effective.

Perhaps an exception to this general statement should be made in the case of the junior college. It is possible but rather unusual for a junior college to develop an alumni organization in the same way as four-year institutions. The time spent in a junior college is comparatively brief, and many of those who finish junior college go on to higher institutions, where they develop their more permanent associations. Still, a great many students come from the community in which the junior college is situated and will go back to that community; they are important members of the public called upon to support the junior college from year to year. Thus, an effort to constitute some alumni relations may not be in vain.

Higher education has a great stake in all alumni. With increasing numbers of people enrolled in higher education, they will in time become the majority of the electorate. Their weight and influence can be decisive in protecting higher education and in making certain that its just needs are met.

Trustee policy should seek to strengthen the ties of alumni to their institution. To this end the institution should keep the alumni informed of current achievements, discoveries, student life, and problems on campus and periodically bring the alumni back to the campus.

Parents

With the virtual emancipation of the young at the age of eighteen, it might appear that parents have no place in higher education. Nothing could be farther from the truth.

Just because a young person has the vote does not mean that he is independent of family or wants to be. The leap from high school to college is still considerable for a great many students. A crowded college campus may be a lonely place. The privilege of self-direction implies problems and responsibilities. The procurement of adequate living facilities can prove troublesome. There comes a time when a freshman needs a friend, even if it is his own parent.

Parents should be encouraged to visit the campus in order to obtain a clearer idea of its objectives and of its impact on their sons and daughters. They should understand better the framework in which their child is growing into emotional and intellectual maturity. They may then be more supportive of their son or daughter and of the institution.

The reverse may also occur. One look at the campus may convince the parents that they will be certain to lose their child "in all the confusion." Father may be mighty upset when he sees the mass of students lolling around the student union. But most parents who have the opportunity will enjoy being oriented—a procedure that should be accomplished with some formality. Parents should receive a guided tour of the campus—more in terms of its academic purposes and plans than its geography. The family should know what it is paying for. When a student has personal problems, it is good to have the assistance of parents. Some knowledge of what occurs on the campus may narrow the generation gap. Indeed, parents may be attracted to attend extension courses offered by the college, thereby to some extent keeping abreast of the education of their children.

The same kind of publication should be sent to parents as is sent to alumni, and some kind of associate membership with the alumni should be made available in order to accomplish this purpose.

Trustee policy should encourage the orientation of parents to the campus scene.

Media

Like other institutions, the university or college has a public image. Sometimes it is the general image presented by fiction or movies, but usually it is more specific: it may reflect the personality of the president, it may appear as a battle ground of student unrest, it may be pictured as a mysterious laboratory in which Nobel laureates spin plans for the future.

In most instances, the media prefer to take the usual course of presenting the bizarre and the dramatic: the co-ed victim of a sex crime; the policeman subduing a student amidst violent protest; anger at a rally; obscene signs at the president's inauguration. College public relations officers try their best to present a different story, a more realistic and constructive story, but often without much success. Research achievements, long hours of study, exchanges in the classroom, the vital processes of growing up intellectually— these do not make good news stories. It is almost impossible to present the day-to-day work of a university, and perhaps it is a mistake to try. But the effort must be made to show higher education in some perspective so that the public does not lose faith in it. During the late sixties the public became disenchanted with higher education and showed its opposition by refusing to vote bond issues for capital improvements and by reducing the amount of its gifts to both private and public institutions.

Trustees can be instrumental in securing fairer press coverage for their institution by pointing out to editors the kinds of subjects worth investigation by reporters and feature writers: such subjects may include curriculum innovations, both those that have worked and those that have failed; study or aid projects for disadvantaged students that are producing positive results; special programs for improving relations between campus and community (for example, a special course for police officers on understanding social conditions, psychological problems in the ghetto, and student attitudes).

Other newsworthy topics may be research which gives new insights into ancient civilizations or new contributions to solving scientific, health, and social problems. A trustee can alert the press to the development of techniques for more effective teaching, effects of increased student participation in decision making, instances of how disciplines relate to each other, and, of course, the statistics of education (there is always a fascination to numbers—admissions, graduates, women lawyers, dollars spent, and so on). Trustees will think of many others that have impressed them in their own institution.

Why should trustees attempt to point out these matters? Because their interest illustrates their own commitment to higher education and may be persuasive to media executives. What deeply interests a lay trustee may well interest an editor. Even better for the institution, however, is if a newspaper editor or television executive sits on the board.

Trustees can also be helpful in arranging conferences with the press and television and radio broadcasters. The media are usually eager to talk over policy problems and background information with the authorities in charge of higher education. The administrative heads of the university or college should be the main participants in these discussions. In such meetings the whole question of a balanced presentation of life on the campus may be brought out. Higher education has become too important in the public mind and too expensive for the public pocketbook for the media to leave it alone to pursue its affairs quietly. The university cannot rely on official handouts on matters such as student demonstrations, faculty protests, important changes in board policy, or exercises of presidential authority. News stories are bound to break out on a large campus, and the better the media understand the campus program and operations, the better chance the institution has for fair treatment. In important situations, however, the institution should speak through a single voice, usually that of the president. In day-to-day relationships the university public information office will be the spokesman.

One arrangement that will assist the university in its coverage by television is an agreement with the stations that they will report news, not create it. In the late sixties it was not unusual for protesting students and television camera crews to have an understanding that nothing much exciting would happen until the cameras arrived and then the protest scenario would be played with gusto. If the cameras had not been dispatched, the chances in many cases were that the action would have been perfunctory.

Finally, the university can make good use of educational television, whether operated by itself or by a community agency. Professors of political science, history, and economics who appear on public affairs programs contribute to public understanding and to university prestige. Universities have not begun to mine the rich store of materials that can advise the public, in an interesting and provocative fashion, what is meant by investigating the past and the present and planning for the future. The university is in the best position to provide a picture of its varied campus life. It should not be afraid to do so.

Of course, when a university engages in teaching directly through the media, as in the case of the "university without walls," it is displaying some phases of its teaching purposes and techniques for all to see and share. Experience has shown that a television-prepared lecture is usually of better quality (at least more structured) than that given in the classroom; there is no time to stutter or to improvise. But something is lost in the process unless arrangements are made for two-way communications, with students calling in questions.

Trustees should make a special effort to interest the communications media in the positive side of higher education. Implementation of such a program will depend upon administration, faculty, and students. Teaching through television provides a showcase.

General Public

Trustees of public institutions know that the public is not happy with higher education. The popular feeling is that the universities and colleges have let them down. The riots of the sixties have not been forgotten. Students, faculty, administrators, and trustees are suspect. Why should so much of the shrinking tax dollar be devoted to their activities? Is higher education preparing students for society or to repudiate it?

Much needs to be done to bring together the institution and its public supporters. More needs to be done to adjust the institution's concept of society. Many of the younger faculty continue to be alienated, partly due to ideology, partly to ignorance of the world outside the campus. It is essential to bring the establishment and the campus together. Businessmen, lawyers, farmers, union leaders, government representatives, and human relations specialists should be invited to participate occasionally in assemblies or classroom discussions about their work. In turn, off-campus visits in these areas may have further advantages.

There are a host of thoughtful, articulate members of the establishment who can give students and faculty a perspective of the marketplace that they are unlikely to receive from their own or conventional sources. Students hear the word "corporation" and they shudder. (This is strange since, as we have seen, the original word *universitas* meant a corporation.) They should see a corporation executive in the flesh and hear him on corporate problems, personnel, practices, social responsibilities, and operational changes. Many large corporations do a better job in providing for upward mobility and opportunities for advancement than does higher education itself. Lawyers know the shortcomings of the administration of justice and what is being done and not being done to rectify them. Government representatives deal every day with the problems of the poor and disadvantaged that trouble the young. The achievements of American society in recent years to provide social security, protect against defrauding the public, prevent hunger, extend health services, provide for old age, ensure equal treatment in employment, protect the environment, subsidize housing, supply purchasing power and credit, though of course far from completed, as Mr. Nader will testify, are astounding.

But the greatest reason for misunderstanding between the campus and the community is that the latter thinks the university is not giving it a fair break. The community does not ask to be shielded against criticism, but it is tired of what it considers to be a one-sided presentation of facts. In other words, the public believes that the university has forsaken its obligation to seek the truth, that it gives a clinical diagnosis of society without giving a complete examination of the patient; that faculty are the intellectual instigators of student disruption, cynicism, or, at best, indifference to the social order. The Town may be very unfair in depicting this image of the Gown. But this is the way it goes in many places.

To repair this misconception, to the extent it is one, the faculty should participate more in the life of the marketplace, and the community leaders should become from time to time part of the life of the college. The business schools have been more sensitive to the need for this kind of adjustment than have liberal arts schools and departments. These exchanges may confirm some adverse faculty and student attitudes toward established society and the economic system. This is an acceptable risk in the pursuit of truth. Nor is it suggested here that the university give up its role as critic of society—only that society be satisfied that the university is presenting all the facts.

Trustee policy should encourage faculty to bring leaders of business, professions, labor, and government to the institution, when the subject matter is pertinent, in order to develop a better understanding between campus and community.

16

MULTI-INSTITUTIONAL, COORDINATING, SUPERBOARDS

The trend in public higher education is unquestionably toward a greater centralization of control. The self-governing individual institution is becoming increasingly rare.

Multiversity boards are constituted to govern a number of institutions. The old-line university has been expanded by the creation of branch campuses; the more recent universities—that is, the successors to the four-year liberal arts colleges, which in turn derived from the normal schools—have been gathered together to form a new system under a single board. In a number of instances, the multiversity systems in turn have been subordinated to a superboard (as in New York, Michigan). In others, a consolidated board has been created to operate all institutions (Oregon, Utah). In still other instances, all senior institutions and some junior or specialized institutions have been consolidated under a single operating board (University of Wisconsin).

Proposals have also been made to cluster universities and colleges on a regional basis in order to share resources—libraries, faculty, space—with a university at the center and four-year and junior colleges as coordinate and feeder institutions. This may be organizationally feasible under a cluster board, but it is likely to provide a geopolitical mess, with regional rivalries focusing on the legislature.

Even when the junior colleges are grouped separately, they are frequently gathered together on a district or regional basis with their own chancellor and board administering a number of campuses. In turn all of the junior college districts or regions are sometimes tied together by a central state junior college coordinating or advisory board. Junior college districts retain a good measure of independence because most of them are, in substantial part, locally financed.

In any event, by one road or another, in varying degrees, public institutions are advancing (some fear retreating) into a form of centralized control.

Number of Campuses under One Board

How many institutions should a board govern? If a super-board, system board, or cluster board exists, should each institution under it also have its own board?

Some believe that five to nine campuses are all one board should govern, in the interest of efficiency and of maintaining contact with the campuses. This is a conservative approach. Many boards govern twenty or more institutions. Effective relationships depend partly on the diversity of the institutions. If all institutions in the system are university branches or four-year colleges, an increase in the number of campuses may be assimilated without too much difficulty, even though individual institutions vary considerably among themselves in emphasis or specialization. Over twenty-five seems beyond reasonable governance; when there is great diversity less than twenty-five may be appropriate.

The justification for systemwide boards is that there are many aspects of administration and policy which should be centralized so as to provide a statewide balance of offerings, avoid needless duplication, and effect economies and good planning. So long as the board of trustees is an operating board, establishing policies for a reasonable number of constituent institutions, it seems best that general policy be determined by a single board, which may mean a single board for each manageable system. If, however, a board is merely a budget and granting agency and cannot possibly determine detailed policies for its institutions (as in the case of the Regents of the State of New York), then each separate institution or system of institutions should have its own board. In short, where the multi-institutional operation becomes so large that meaningful governance by a particular board becomes impossible, the governance should be divided on a state system, regional, or local basis as experience or study indicate. Once the proper unit of governance is determined, however, all of the considerations relating to the selection of board representation apply.

The number of campuses a single board can govern depends on manageability, which in turn depends on diversity. More campuses can be gathered under a single board if the missions (though not their methods) are essentially the same.

Headquarters and Meeting Places

An immediate problem for a new system (and sometimes for an older one) is where to establish its headquarters. Should they be on one of the campuses or away from any campus? Should they be in the state capital so that there is maximum accessibility for and to government officials?

It is better to locate headquarters outside of the state capital, for there will be sufficient political pressures without inviting more. The headquarters should at least be a symbol of the educational independence of the federation of institutions. It seems sensible to establish the headquarters in an area close to a concentration of campuses operated by the system, or perhaps close to headquarters for coordinate systems[1] with which it is essential to cooperate in

---

[1] Such as (1) university of the state, (2) state colleges, (3) central senior college board.

matters of educational policy. The educational capital should be kept outside of the political capital, if possible.

It also appears preferable to locate the headquarters outside of any particular campus of the system. To have the board of trustees and president of the entire system located on a particular campus tends to diminish the stature and independence of the administration of that campus. It is inevitable that the central headquarters will become unnecessarily involved in the particular problems of the campus in which the headquarters are located.

Where should the system's board of trustees meet? The first impulse is to meet on the various campuses constituting the system. Within reasonable limits this should be done if for no other reason than to acquaint the institution with the fact that there is a board of trustees. But transportation problems may make it difficult to meet on a different campus each time; too much time may be lost going to and from the institution.

Moreover, a trustee may not be able to savor the flavor of the campus as he would like. When his time schedule is tight, he flies and drives to a large conference room in one of the campus buildings, and when the meeting is over he tries to take the first plane home. He might as well be at an airport hotel or at the system headquarters off campus in a neutral area. Even if he stays overnight near the campus, and is honored at dinner by the community and entertained by the campus glee club, he will not see much of the campus or be able to talk to its faculty and students.

In a multiple institution system, the better procedure usually is to provide for general board meetings at off-campus places easily accessible by air or car (unless the system consists of institutions close together, as in New York City and in the Boston area). Then, twice a year, trustees may go to campuses for special meetings extended to include scheduled conferences about local problems with campus administrators, faculty, and students, although the bulk of campus inquiry should be left to board committees that can make separate in-depth visits.

Headquarters of a multiversity should be located away from any particular campus, but not in the state capital.

Multiversity boards should usually meet at headquarters or convenient transportation junctions (such as airports), but the board committees should meet on the various campuses.

Decentralization

A difficult administrative question is how much a university or college system with a number of institutions—as in California, Illinois, Michigan, New York, North Carolina—should decentralize. The prevailing practice is for the president of the system to propose campus presidential or chancellor appointments to the central board for approval, involving board members in the selection process. (The selection committee should include representatives of the campus faculty and central administration, probably the president of one of the sister campuses, and it may include a student or two.) The campus president or chancellor is an agent of the central system. But he also may be the head of an institution with fifty or one hundred years of history, well established in the community, with a proud tradition of its own. To what extent should the system decentralize authority to the local president and campus?

Obviously, the headquarters office must retain control over the total budget of the local campus, the overall admission policies to the extent they relate to an overall plan, basic personnel practices, the introduction of costly new academic programs and capital outlays. But once the central office is satisfied with respect to local accountability, it should permit the campus to operate as freely as legally possible within its budget allocation—leaving most problems of faculty status (appointments, tenure, and so on) and educational and administrative operations to the particular institution. Similar delegation should apply to changes within the basic curriculum (as approved by the central administration) and intrabudgetary transfers. The institution should be given sufficient flexibility to meet its own requirements and respond to its particular demands. An institution of 5,000 to 20,000 students should have an identity, a life, and a responsibility of its own.

The question arises whether the local institution requires its own Board of Trustees in order to procure a sufficient measure of delegation. In New York, where the central Board of Regents has the entire educational structure of the state under its jurisdiction, it is clear that delegation or statutory allocation is required to subsystems with their own boards, such as the State University of New York, the City University of New York, and a number of independent institutions. In North Carolina, the higher education law provides for both central and institutional boards and in broad outline delineates their functions (the delegation to the local boards is mostly to ensure compliance with the policies of the Central Board of Governors regarding personnel, curriculum, research, and public services).

Both the University of California and the California State University and Colleges operate without local boards, although the latter provides, under statute, for advisory boards to the local college president. Local policy boards can introduce a competitive element toward the procurement of funds, a provincialism and divisiveness which are not desirable. Use of an advisory board, which the local campus president appoints on the approval of the central board, straddles the issue, and it has worked out reasonably well in the California State University and Colleges. These boards have built up community interest in the institutions for gifts and other community-related purposes, and have been especially effective for colleges in nonmetropolitan areas. Delegation to the local campus can be effected without the insertion of another policy-making layer, and probably most local presidents and faculties would prefer that such power be delegated to them, rather than to a local board. Local policy and operating boards may also increase rather than decrease the number of contacts with and burdens upon the central board. Moreover, a group of institutions unified under one board will have more of an advantage vis-à-vis the governor and the legislature. Whether local operating boards, advisory boards, or no local boards work best depends on a state's history and experience with higher education, but a system of too many diverse units under a single umbrella must decentralize to subsystem or local boards.

An administrative problem that occasionally arises is the nature and scope of the delegation of authority. Suppose the president of a multiversity, with board approval, delegates some of his authority to the chancellor of a local campus. May that chancellor in turn redelegate the authority to a dean or department head? This was one of the problems in connection with the reappointment of Angela Davis as a UCLA assistant professor of philosophy. The UCLA chancellor had been given the power to appoint and reappoint, but there was a question as to whether he had redelegated, in practical effect, down to the department level. This question was rendered moot by Miss Davis' involvement in her trial, although the Regents meanwhile revoked any delegation of authority to the chancellor to appoint in her case. The wisdom of such revocation of delegation of authority is not the point considered here, but simply that administrative delegation should be clearly defined in terms of the office to which it is delegated or whether it may be redelegated and, if so, to whom.

Under usual circumstances it is inadvisable to set up local policy and operating boards within a system. If such boards are established, they should have well-defined responsibilities in relation to the central board.

Delegation of authority to staff should be defined in scope, particularly whether it can be redelegated and to whom.

Coordinating Council

In the 1960s, the public institutions—universities, colleges, and junior colleges—expanded at a phenomenal rate, more than doubling their student population. Alarmed state finance departments, legislators, and educational groups recognized that needless duplication of services must be avoided and that educational resources had to be organized and rationalized for most effective use. The principal way of doing so was to create a state coordinating council for higher education.

The theory of coordination was that the top representatives of multiversity systems could resolve their differences if they met in a public forum in the presence of representatives from the general public and private institutions, who would also be full-fledged members of the council. Through the exchange of information, plans, and ideas, the council would control orderly expansion—by approving new campuses and programs, by commenting on the general levels of support budgets, by taking an overall statesmanlike view on planning for all segments, and by gathering and distributing pertinent manpower and educational data of common concern. The council could then advise the systems, the governor, and the legislature on the proper courses of action.

However, the coordinating council has been criticized as being ineffectual. When the major systems were in disagreement, their representatives supposedly obstructed action by block voting, and compelled the public members unhappily to abstain or choose sides. When the representatives agreed, which was most of the time, the council was accused of encouraging logrolling. When the advice of the council was contrary to the policy of a major system, the advice was politely circumvented or disregarded. Changes in council membership—reducing the number of system representatives and increasing the number of public representatives—did not accomplish any basic reforms. This record demonstrates, apparently, that an advisory body can be effective only if its advice is customarily and traditionally accepted and if it deliberates and acts independently.

The success of a coordinating council largely depends on its director and staff. The personnel engaged in research and planning must at least be the equal of their counterparts in the systems they advise. If the multiversity staffs are served by highly paid research and scholarly personnel and the council staff must be civil service, the council's status is compromised before it starts—unless the civil service permits professional employees in this specialized area to be most generously compensated. However, it may help the council even more if its professional employees are exempt from civil service.

With an able and respected staff, a coordinating council can do much to bring about a rational use of educational resources throughout the state. Much of the coordination can be achieved by bringing together the staffs of the various educational systems under neutral professional auspices. Disputes or misunderstandings often can be resolved on such administrative levels when the problems are identified, though the council must reserve the right for its staff and itself to make independent evaluations.

Sometimes it is difficult for an interested system to yield to council advice. But a tradition of acceptance must be established, or the legislature will not continue to support the council. (The United Nations Security Council cannot be the model of a coordinating council for higher education—sovereignty is too jealously guarded.) The broad-gauged planning of the coordinating council, arrived at after consultation with the systems, must provide these systems and the legislature with effective guidelines for setting up or abolishing programs. (However, the systems should be able to try out two- or three-year innovative programs without council approval.) The trustees of multiversity systems must decide for themselves whether they prefer to abide by coordinating council decisions or to risk the establishment of a superboard or a single consolidated board. The legislature, by supporting and implementing council recommendations, thus giving it prestige, can do more than any other agency to ensure the success of the council.

A coordinating council of multiversity systems can be effective only if it can employ an independent, respected staff, and only if its recommendations are customarily carried out by the systems and supported by the legislature.

Superboards

A state may prefer a superboard—made up entirely of public members—whose policy decisions will be mandatory upon its operating boards or subordinate institutions. North Carolina has such an agency to allocate educational resources and determine programs, and the institutional boards may act only in areas not reserved to the superboard. In California and in several other states such an organization could be set up only by a state constitutional amendment.

It remains to be seen whether this structure represents sound educational policy and how adaptable it is to the conditions in other states. New York, for example, has long had such a board, and indeed the Regents of New York establish certain policies for all education, public and private, from kindergarten through higher education. No school of music can be chartered without a grant by the Regents, and a vast number of other institutions, even in higher education, fall within their jurisdiction. But the Regents can do very little administration or supervision. The State University of New York and the City University of New York have their own boards, and the extent of regents' control is minimal. In fact, in actual impact on higher education, the New York Regents may be less effective than many coordinating councils.

The question is how much a board can do. To operate or supervise a myriad of different institutions is nearly impossible; such a board can issue general guidelines and allocate money, but that is about all. Of course, if the superboard is given a grant of funds to reallocate among its constituent systems and institutions, it will have considerable power over the direction of education by its control over funding. It can plan for the state as a whole and in general terms control the implementation of the plan by its budgetary allocations.

As the institutions become fewer and more homogeneous, the opportunity for effective direction by a superboard increases. Its effectiveness must be measured by how it enforces its directives, what sanctions it can and does apply. In a case where a superboard does function, unless broad powers remain in the systems or in the individual institutions, their system or institutional boards will lose in prestige. Probably the most effective superboard is one of specific but limited powers that enable it to deal with centralized planning, allocation of total grants, and approval of new campuses and major programs.

A superboard can be effective only if it supervises a manageable group of systems and institutions and if it can enforce its sanctions.

Consolidated Boards

In a few instances, states have decided against the idea of several boards supervised by a superboard and have created a consolidated board to directly administer all public institutions (the vocational may be excepted). Either a single new board is created or an old one retained to merge all prior boards. The board is intended to be the governing agency of the higher education conglomerate.

An example of such consolidation is the Wisconsin Board of Higher Education, which represents a merger of the University of Wisconsin, the Wisconsin State University, and a number of two-year institutions that are branches of the university system. In all it consists of approximately seventeen branches. The consolidation is too new to provide many answers to the questions of higher education governance. It is reported to be still in a state of "chaotic transition."

Undoubtedly the Wisconsin board will have its problems. Can the recipient of so many legacies be fair to them and to the educational process? Will the trustees lean toward the protection of the research-oriented university and subordinate the four-year institutions to second-class treatment? Will they favor the teaching concept of the four-year schools and dilute the quality of the old university? What will they do with the junior colleges whose "junior" designation is now deleted? The pressures that were formerly competing in the legislature will be competing within the total system. The question is, how viable will such a complex system be and how much variety can survive and live well in a single system?

Another, perhaps more difficult example relates to the University of Rhode Island. There the regents have authorization over all public and elementary schools and higher education; they receive the grants of educational funds and distribute them to the respective institutions. Many of the conflicts in the Wisconsin situation exist here, augmented by the competing demands of the public school system. A single board cannot be expected to administer effectively with such diversity.

A consolidated board's main problem is how to deal fairly with institutional diversity.

Regional Boards and Consortiums

Regional boards would govern a university and junior and specialized institutions within a geographic region. The theory is that they would bring together the educational resources of a region and encourage rational and reciprocal uses of resources.

It is quite true that private institutions such as the Claremont Colleges and institutions in the Boston area have formed effective federations and have complemented each other's programs. But public clusters have not followed suit, and the reason seems clear: the state becomes divided into educational provinces that bring competing pressures upon the legislature, which intensify the political struggle for educational resources.

However, there is a growing recognition that institutions both public and private within a region can supplement each other's programs, make courses available to students from the other institutions, and share library and laboratory resources. Through voluntary consortiums, they are accomplishing much sharing of resources. But their motivation is mutual benefit, particularly for the students enrolled in the respective institutions. The control of the competitive element is not the motivation. The effectiveness of consortiums will probably increase as public funds in one form or other are made

available to private institutions and public funding is given on a
condition that resources within the geographic area be shared to the
fullest extent possible.

*Regional consortiums are meeting with success; regional
cluster boards are likely to be engaged in troublesome competition
for statewide resources.*

General Considerations

Most of the considerations that apply to the selection qualifications and balance of a single board apply to the selection qualifications and balance of a superboard or coordinating board. It may
be more important, however, that many members of these highly
centralized boards have prior experience on other higher education
boards than is usually the case of board appointments. In order to be
able to establish policy for a multiplicity and variety of institutions,
the trustee should have some idea how they operate and what the
problems are close to the campus. The experience factor becomes
most important.

Faculty and students already are inclined to look upon
multiversity (system) boards as absentee boards, and the superboard
or consolidated board is even more remote. But, paradoxically, it
may develop that the further away the decision-making power is
based, the more local power (in the day-to-day operations) will be
reasserted by the campus president and faculty, because someone has
to be minding the store.

Personally, I believe that just as there is a need for a balanced
board, so is there a need for balanced centers of power in the governance of higher education. Too much centralization will result in
an uncontrolled and unmeasured bureaucracy. Competition in
higher education is not to be shunned if it can be regulated and
guided. The drives for excellence can be made on different levels
and for different purposes. These may be lost if the educational program becomes overcentralized.

The reverse is that the drives for excellence can be frustrated
if the educational program becomes too decentralized. The state
does require coordination in higher education to create effective new
programs and to avoid waste. The coordinating council voluntarily
supported by the related segments and by the legislature could still

provide the best answer, but it takes statesmanship to carry it out. In any event, this conclusion seems true for California, where a three-tiered master plan for higher education provided an effective model for many years but where the program has been seriously questioned by the legislature. Centralized planning along broad lines that will be adhered to is the essential matter; operations should follow historical and evolutionary patterns.

In practice a coordinating council whose recommendations on planning, expansion, and new programs are customarily followed by the legislature and the constituent systems is little different from a board where determinations in these areas are mandatory. But the advisory relationship provides for more interchange and flexibility and guards against bureaucratic controls.

New Development in Coordination

A most interesting development in coordination in California formulates a different pattern for the appointment of trustees and provides for a new commission, entitled "The California Post Secondary Education Commission," to succeed to all the functions previously vested in the Coordinating Council for Higher Education.

It is still essentially an advisory board—to the governor, the legislature, government officials, and institutions of postsecondary education—but its authority is strengthened two ways: by the method of appointment of its members and through a detailed statement of functions. It has twenty-three members, twelve of whom are public lay members and the remainder ex officio lay members. Of the twelve appointed members, eight are selected by the legislature (four by the Senate Rules Committee and four by the speaker of the assembly) and four are selected by the governor. The extent of appointing power given to the legislative branch is unusual.

The eleven ex officio members are selected from the regents of the University of California, the trustees of the California State University and Colleges, the Board of Governors of the California Community Colleges, the independent (private) California colleges and universities (appointment by the governor from an association list), the chairmen of councils dealing with vocational education and private postsecondary institutions (two from each), and the president of the State Board of Education or his designee. The governor appoints many of these other board members so there is a greater balance between executive and legislative appointments than may first appear.

However, control of coordination and of centralized planning is clearly given to a lay board. The presidents and chancellors of the institutions are not included as members, but they, along with the superintendent of public instruction, are placed on an advisory committee to the board. The theory appears to be that the chief executive officers of the institutions to be coordinated exercise too much influence on their colleagues if they are members of the board. It remains to be seen whether they will have a similar weighty influence as advisers. Though these prestigious and persuasive educational leaders are excluded, their podium for advocacy as advisers may be more potent than their seats at the table.

The commission has these duties: to require the governing boards of the segments of public postsecondary education to develop long-range plans; to write a five-year state plan which integrates or adjusts these various plans; and, in connection with such planning, to consider the need for and location of new facilities, the programs appropriate to each system, budgetary procedures, student charges, admissions, programs of private institutions, and differentiating functions of the public segments. It is to up-date the plan annually, advise the executive and legislative branches as to whether segmental budget requests are compatible with the state plan, advise them on the need for new institutions and programs, identify societal and educational needs, encourage change and innovation, conduct studies of projected manpower supply, make recommendations regarding adult and continuing education, and in general act as a clearinghouse for postsecondary information and policy recommendations. Significantly, the act establishing the commission contains several sections on legislative intention which state that all actions requiring state appropriations will not be authorized unless recommended by the new commission.

This organization was not accidentally or impulsively come by. It followed two years of careful investigation by a legislative committee and the receipt of a report (supporting a much more conventional structure) from a statewide citizens' committee.[1] The legislature concluded that it would place more faith in the advice of a board of trustees which, in large part, reflected its own choice of personnel. Whether this appointment procedure will have the anticipated result remains to be seen. Whether the governor will be receptive to recommendations made by a board substantially selected by the legislature also remains to be seen. If the quality of board membership is high, irrespective of the source of the appointment, and if the board reaches agreement on the important issues, it could become a very powerful agency. Advice which is respected by the executive and legislative departments of government and relating to the basic allocation of resources, planning, and budget can be most effective even with respect to a constitutional body such as the University of California, which must turn to the legislature for funds. But if this new commission becomes politically controlled or inspired or if cleavages develop between the general public board members and the lay board members of the segments, the purposes of coordination will have received a heavy blow. If this organizational structure meets with success, it may pioneer new pathways for higher education, and trustees of consolidated boards, superboards, or subsystems in California and in other states may be selected along similar appointive lines. Speculation concerning this new educational ship of state could be endless, and proof of its sea-worthiness must await experience.

Advance reports of the third Newman Task Force Report to the HEW on the "federal role" state that the Newman Committee expresses considerable concern about state coordination in higher education. The committee believes that such coordination can result in a kind of nonprofit conglomerate which should be subject to federal regulation on some antitrust basis. In other words coordination can give undue support to uniformity, to standardization of curricula and credentials, to educational cost accounting, to limitation of access, to the prevention of diversity and competition. The

---

[1] The new commission embodies several principles recommended by Lyman Glenny and associates in *Coordinating Higher Education for the 70s*—to wit, a majority of lay members unconnected with any board; a presidential and other advisory committees; and broad coordinating functions.

federal role should be to provide incentives for competition and diversity, particularly for channeling federal aid to students (perhaps utilizing the coordinating agency, but giving institutional aid only to the institutions which the students select to attend). The student, as consumer, will control the competition.

The validity of these assumptions is open to debate. Coordination is necessary on a state level, but is not a necessary evil. The state can be just as interested in diversity, through coordination, as can the federal government; indeed, it can be far more effective in this area. It knows its institutions better than Washington and certainly as well as its freshman students. There are dangers in coordination that becomes bureaucratic and centralized. But when a necessary function of government has to be performed, it is not valid to oppose it or predicate policy against it on the ground that it may be abused. Most trustees will probably endorse the principle of direct student aid, providing student choice within limits, but federal policy should not leave the survival and health of public institutions entirely to the unpredictable and varying exercises of student options. With well over a hundred years of aid experience behind it, the federal government should be able directly or through the coordinating agency to provide institutional aid where it is required, and public trustees generally may be expected to endorse this position.

Legislature and Governor

No matter what independence a system of institutions may have on paper, even embodied in the state constitution, the power of the purse can provide a strong element of control. Public universities and colleges need friends in the legislature and executive branch more than ever.

In years past, the legislature and governor were generous to all higher education and to the old-line universities in particular, which were trusted like the old University of Paris, the "daughter of the king." But the universities and colleges, for many reasons not entirely of their own making, presented a bedraggled picture to the legislatures during the sixties and have lost some of their cultural sanctity; they have become another set of competitors for the tax dollar.

At present, state legislatures seem to be favoring career-oriented programs. To keep an independent balance, to insist on providing programs and curricula with more intangible values, will demand the closest attention of higher education boards, no matter how organized.

EPILOGUE

USES AND ABUSES OF THE TRUSTEESHIP

A board of trustees of a public university and college has many uses. It may be a forum for the discussion of educational policy for the public to witness, a sounding board for administration and faculty, and a control mechanism to require the administration to plan and deal with priorities. It selects the chief executive and stimulates innovation and change.

It is the representative of the public responding to the demands and aspirations of the institution; the representative of the institution advising its various publics and government of institutional needs, projects, and purposes; the procurer of public and private funding; and supporter of faculty status, educational quality,

223

and academic freedom. It is an agency prepared to deal sympathetically with youth and youth's problems, to listen to students and to speak to them frankly, to understand their impatience with an imperfect world, to promote and approve policies that treat them as mature people, capable of being responsible, and holding them to responsibility.

The board must be conscious that it holds much of the legal power of governance but know that it can succeed only through the wise sharing of that power with administration, faculty, and students. It must believe in its trust, in its particular mission within the many goals of higher education. It must know that in its hands rests much of the future of the noblest secular institution created by Western civilization, an instrument that is as complex and fragile as the human mind is complex and fragile. The board must protect the university against those who would weaken it from without by overeconomizing in the support budget, by limiting its scope of experimentation, by restricting its freedom to pursue the truth, and by shifting too much authority to political centers. It must defend the university against those who would try to weaken it from within by pressuring to homogenize faculty, to disregard merit, to act as though democratic government cannot provide procedures to afford equal opportunity and yet reward excellence, and to reconstitute it to serve political purposes. There is much to be done by trustees who take their assignment seriously.

Of course, there are abuses of power which a board of trustees must avoid: too much engagement in administration; too much second-guessing of the president; too much delay in dealing with faculty and student grievances; too much squabbling about minor matters; too much insistence that the institution be operated as a business; too much effort to act *in loco parentis;* too little understanding and exchange with faculty; too little sympathy with the needs of students; too little homework on developing issues; too little firmness when firmness may be required; too much evasion of responsibility; too passive a position in the face of pressure.

But when the uses and abuses of trustees are weighed, I suspect that the trustee boards' overall record in recent years shows a positive contribution to the cause of higher education, that trustees are not an anachronism in college and university government and that, strengthened by a more carefully selected and diverse representation, they will see their institutions through the challenge of the remaining years of this changing century.

RELEVANT
READINGS

The following list contains readings I have found useful or provocative concerning trustees and the problems they confront. It is illustrative of material that is available and is not intended as a comprehensive bibliography.

Books

BECK, H. P. *Men Who Control Our Universities*. New York: King's Crown Press, 1947.

BURNS, G. P. *Trustees in Higher Education*. New York: Independent College Funds of America, 1966.

CORSON, J. J. *Governance of Colleges and Universities*. New York: McGraw-Hill, 1962.

EURICH, A. C. (Ed) *Campus 1980*. New York: Dell, 1968.

GERTH, D. R., HAEHN, J. O., AND ASSOCIATES. *An Invisible Giant: The California State Colleges*. San Francisco: Jossey-Bass, 1971.

GLENNY, L. A., BERDAHL, R. O., PALOLA, E. G., AND PALTRIDGE, J. A. *Coordinating Higher Education for the 70's*. Berkeley: Center for Research and Development in Higher Education, University of California, 1971.

226

HERRON, U. R., JR. *The Role of the Trustee*. New York: Intext, 1969.

HODGKINSON, H. L., AND MEETH, L. R. (Eds.) *Power and Authority: Transformation of Campus Governance*. San Francisco: Jossey-Bass, 1971.

HUGHES, R. *A Manual for Trustees of Colleges and Universities*. Ames, Iowa: Collegiate Press, 1945.

KERR, C. *The Uses of the University*. New York: Harper and Row, 1966.

LEE, E. C., AND BOWEN, F. M. *The Multi Campus University*. New York: McGraw-Hill, 1971. (Particularly Ch. 4.)

MC CONNELL, T. R. *The Redistribution of Power in Higher Education*. Berkeley: Center for Research and Development in Higher Education, University of California, 1971.

MC GRATH, E. J. *Should Students Share the Power?* Philadelphia: Temple University Press, 1970.

MILLETT, J. D. *The Academic Community*. New York: McGraw-Hill, 1962.

MORTORANA, S. V. *College Boards of Trustees*. New York: Center for Applied Research in Education, 1963.

NEWSOM, C. V. *A University President Speaks Out*. New York: Harper and Row, 1961.

NICHOLS, D. C. (Ed.) *Perspectives on Campus Tensions*. Washington, D.C.: American Council on Education, 1970. (Includes chapter by J. L. Zwingle on the lay governing board.)

PERKINS, J. A. (Ed.) *Higher Education: From Autonomy to Systems*. New York: International Council for Educational Development, 1972.

RASHDALL, H. *The Universities of Europe in the Middle Ages*. New York: Oxford University Press, 1936. (Vol. I, Ch. 4; Vol. II, Chs. 6 and 10.)

RAUH, M. A. *Trusteeship of Colleges and Universities*. New York: McGraw-Hill, 1969.

RUML, B., AND MORRISON, D. *Memo to a College Trustee*. New York: McGraw-Hill, 1959.

Reports

BABBIDGE, H. D., JR. *Eighth Annual Faculty Convocation*. Storrs: University of Connecticut, 1969. (Includes chapter on the role of trustees.)

The California Master Plan for Higher Education in the 70's and Be-

yond. Select Committee Report to California Coordinating Council for Higher Education. Sacramento, 1972.

Carnegie Commission on Higher Education. Various reports (all published by McGraw-Hill, New York), particularly:

The Capitol and the Campus: State Responsibility for Post-secondary Education. 1971.

A Chance to Learn: An Action Agenda for Equal Opportunity in Higher Education. 1970.

Higher Education: Who Pays? Who Benefits? Who Should Pay? 1973.

HODGKINSON, H. L. *Institutions in Transition: A Profile of Change in Higher Education*. 1971.

LADD, D. R. *Change in Educational Policy: Self-Studies in Selected Colleges and Universities*. 1970.

Less Time More Options: Education Beyond the High School. 1970.

PERKINS, J. A. *The University as an Organization*. Chs. 10–13. 1973.

SPURR, S. H. *Academic Degree Structures: Innovative Approaches, Principles of Reform in Degree Structures in the United States*. 1970.

Commission on Academic Tenure in Higher Education. *Faculty Tenure*. San Francisco: Jossey-Bass, 1973.

Final Report of the Assembly Advisory Council on Public Employee Relations. Benjamin Aaron, Chairman. Sacramento: State of California, 1973.

FISHER, B. C. *Duties and Responsibilities of College and University Trustees*. Raleigh: North Carolina Board of Higher Education, 1969.

Fourth Interim Reports. New York: Special Committee of the Trustees, Columbia University, 1969.

HARTNETT, R. T. *College and University Trustees: Their Backgrounds, Roles, and Education Attitudes*. Princeton, N.J.: Educational Testing Service, 1969.

HARTNETT, R. T. *The New College Trustee: Some Predictions for the 1970's*. Princeton, N.J.: Educational Testing Service, 1970.

HODGKINSON, H. L. *Student Participation in Governance*. Berkeley: Center for Research and Development in Higher Education, University of California, 1971.

How Big? A Review of Campus Size. Los Angeles: Office of the Chancellor, California State Colleges, 1970.

National Policy and Higher Education. Frank Newman, Chairman. Washington, D.C.: Government Printing Office, 1973.

PALTRIDGE, J. G. *Trustee Decision Making Patterns in Four Year Institutions.* Berkeley: Center for Research and Development in Higher Education, University of California, in press.

Recommendations and Report. Albany: New York State Regents Advisory Committee on Educational Leadership, 1966.

The Report of the President's Commission on Campus Unrest. Washington, D.C.: Government Printing Office, 1970.

Report on Higher Education. Frank Newman, Chairman. Washington, D.C.: Government Printing Office, 1971.

Periodicals

AAUP Bulletin
> *AAUP Policy Documents and Reports.* 1973.
>
> Academic freedom and tenure reports. Most issues.
>
> ADAMS, W. "Tenure Quotas." June 1973.
>
> ALSTYNE, W. V. "The Supreme Court Speaks to the Untenured." September 1972.
>
> BREWSTER, K., JR. "On Tenure." December 1972.
>
> Comparative Faculty Salary Study. Annual. (Also reported in *The Chronicle of Higher Education.*)
>
> DAVIS, B. H. "Unions and Higher Education: Another View." September 1968.
>
> FISKIN, M. W. "Collective Bargaining and University Government." June 1971.
>
> KADISH, S. H. "The Strike and the Professoriate." June 1968.
>
> KADISH, S. H. "The Theory of the Profession and Its Predicament." June 1972.
>
> LEWIS, G. F. "The Slow Road to Student Liberation." December 1971.
>
> "On Collective Bargaining: The Association's New Statement." December 1972.
>
> *Student Protest.* Includes articles by W. D. Maxwell on some dimensions of relevance and by T. R. McConnell on faculty interests in value, change, and power conflicts. September 1969.
>
> "Student Ratings of Faculty." September 1969.
>
> "Surviving the Seventies (Economic Status Report of the Profession)." June 1973.

AGB Reports (Association of Governing Boards, Washington, D.C.)

BABBIDGE, H. D., JR. "An Agenda for Trustees." July 1966.

BYRNE, J. C. "Students and Trustees—Conflict or Community." July 1966.

CORSON, J. J. "The Board of Trustees—Necessity or Anachronism?" July-August 1973.

DOMINGUEZ, J. I. "To Reign or To Rule: A Choice for Trustees." January 1973.

GLENNY, L. A. "The Anonymous Leaders of Higher Education." January 1973.

HENDERSON, A. D. "The Role of the Governing Board." October 1967.

NELSON, C. A. "Trustees: Serve or Resign (Conversation with Clark Kerr)." July-August 1973.

The American Scholar

MULLER, H. J. "Education for the Future." Summer 1972.

MULLER, H. J. "The Relevance of the Humanities." Winter 1971.

Atlantic Monthly

HERRNSTEIN, R. "IQ." September 1971.

Center Magazine (Center for the Study of Democratic Institutions)

MC DONALD, D. "The Carnegie Study of Higher Education." September-October 1973.

Change

"The Case for Open Admissions." Summer 1973.

"Down with the Degree Structure." March 1973.

EYSENCK, H. J. "IQ, Social Class and Educational Policy." September 1973.

LADD, E. C., AND LIPSET, S. M. "Unionizing the Professoriate." Summer 1973.

NISBET, R. "The Future of Tenure." April 1973.

"Two Responses to the Newman Proposals." Winter 1972–1973.

Change Reports

POTTINGER, J. S., AND BUNZEL, J. H. "The Debate Over Quotas."

The Chronicle of Higher Education (Washington, D.C.; published weekly during the academic year with certain exceptions; provides lively news reports on the most important developments in higher education; includes a section entitled "Point of View," pertinent examples from which are listed here)

"The Admissions Mess." September 25, 1972.

BREWSTER, K., JR. "Four Paradoxes in Higher Education and How to Deal with Them." May 22, 1972.

"Finding New Dollars in Old Budgets." May 15, 1972.

"How To Be a Bad College Teacher." June 5, 1972.

"Study Now, Pay Later: Threat to a Great Commitment." December 6, 1971.

WILSON, L. "Six New Doctrines That Send My Blood Pressure Up." January 31, 1972.

Commentary

MAYER, M. "Higher Education for All?" February 1973.

SEABURY, P. "The Idea of Merit." December 1972.

Educational Record

FLENTJE, H. E., AND SAMPLE, S. B. "Statewide Reallocation Through Program Priorities." 1973, *54* (3), 175.

HEYNS, R. W. "Leadership Lessons from Watergate." 1973, *54* (3), 172.

The EPE 15-Minute Reports for College and University Trustees (published by Editorial Projects for Education, Washington, D.C.)

"Academic Job Discrimination: The Federal Position." September 22, 1972.

"Affirmative Action: 'An Overriding Interest'." March 23, 1973.

"Limiting the Ph.D.: High Costs, High Standards." February 16, 1973.

"New Slant on Research: A Threat to Quality?" January 5, 1973.

"State Funds for Higher Education." June 7, 1972.

"Trustees' Decisions: What Is More Important?" March 23, 1973.

Harpers

LIEBERMAN, M. "Professors Unite." October 1971.

The Journal of Higher Education

Organizational Development in Higher Education. 1973, *44* (5).

The External Degree. 1973, *44* (6).

Liberal Education (published by the American Association of Colleges, Washington, D.C.)

BLOUSTEIN, E. J. "On Collective Bargaining in the Halls of Academe." May 1973, 187–193.

O'NEIL, R. M. "The Colleges and the Courts: A Peacetime Perspective." May 1973, 176–186.

Saturday Review

Who Runs the University? Includes an article by W. M. Roth on the dilemmas of leadership. January 10, 1970.

Alumni Magazines

The following are representative of alumni magazines, which bring the achievements and problems of the institution to the alumni:

Brown Alumni Monthly, Brown University
California Monthly, University of California, Berkeley
The UCLA Monthly, University of California, Los Angeles
Harvard Bulletin, Harvard University
Missouri Alumnus, University of Missouri, Columbia
Rutgers Alumni Magazine, Rutgers University
Wisconsin Alumnus, University of Wisconsin
Yale Alumni Magazine, Yale University

INDEX